I0099750

BEING CATHOLIC IN TROUBLED TIMES

STRENGTH THROUGH FAITH

DENNIS ORTMAN, Ph.D.

Copyright 2024 by MSI Press LLC

All rights reserved. No part of this book may be reproduced or utilized in any form or by any means, electronic or mechanical, including photocopying and recording, or by any information storage and retrieval system without permission in writing from the publisher.

For information, contact

MSI Press, LLC

1760-F Airline Hwy #203

Hollister, CA 95023

Copyeditor: Betty Lou Leaver

Cover design & layout: Opeyemi Ikuborije

ISBN: 978-1-957354-48-4

LCCN: 2024943529

CONTENTS

INTRODUCTION

"Rejoice in hope, be patient under trial, persevere in prayer."
—Paul of Tarsus

My whole life troubled people have come to me for counseling.

Over the years, as I moved around, the settings changed, but my work remained the same. People search for meaning in tough times. They try to make sense of it. They often look for support and guidance, which I provide. My role has been to accompany them in their explorations and give them some pointers.

My counseling career began as a Catholic priest. I served in various parishes in the Detroit area for 14 years. My parishioners came to me in crisis and came for confession. I offered them the consolation of the faith and often referred them to a professional psychologist.

When I left the active ministry at age 40 to get married, I pursued studies in clinical psychology to become a psychologist. I loved the work as a priest and wanted to serve others in a similar capacity. I found in my work as a psychologist a way of continuing that service. Again, people come to me in crisis, and we journey together through it and find new life.

I share with my patients what I have personally learned in negotiating the crises in my own life. You cannot give to another what you do not have. For example, in my decision to leave the priesthood I reflected, prayed, and agonized over the decision for several years. I met weekly with a psychologist and regularly with my spiritual director. I begged God for guidance and only left when I believed it was His will that I leave the active ministry. I did not abandon a life of service but only changed its form. I am now pursuing a new vocation.

Over my nearly 30 years of being a psychologist in private practice, my way of doing therapy has changed. I was trained in Freudian psychology, which does not allow a significant place for religion. My calling has been to integrate the first and second halves of my life, to reconcile my theological training with my psychological education. Working with my patients, I noticed how much I have become a spiritual director to them. We search together for ways of quickening their spirit, which is really recognizing and releasing the Spirit of God dwelling within them.

I was born and raised Catholic. I have had my squabbles with the Church and left for a while. But I have always come back home to my faith community. I bring my Catholic outlook to my work without being preachy or trying to convert anyone. The word *catholic* means "including a wide variety of things, all-embracing." Therefore, with my patients we search for the truth wherever it may be found. Sometimes, we discover it hidden in plain sight in unexpected places. For example, in their darkest moments they find new light and life. When they are most in despair, a ray of hope shines through.

For me, being Catholic also means being open-minded to other religious traditions. We Catholics do not have a corner on the truth. The Mystery of God is greater than the capacity of any religious tradition to contain its fullness. However, all the world religions reveal a valuable perspective on the Truth. We can learn from each other. In that spirit, I have explored the Eastern spiritual traditions. I learned that their wisdom complements that of the Catholic faith and enriches my own faith.

I wrote this book as a series of essays during a troubling time in our world, during the pandemic. I often asked my patients how they experienced the mandated social distancing. "Was it more like a prison or a retreat?" I asked. In the beginning, most said it was a retreat. But over time, it has become more like a prison for many as pandemic fatigue set in. The pandemic has been for me a privileged time of retreat, of prayer and reflection. I have focused more than ever on what is really important in my life, on what really lasts. In these essays I share my explorations in finding meaning during these troubling times. Having a catholic outlook, I draw on the wisdom of many spiritual traditions.

I invite you to reflect with me in reading these essays to deepen your understanding during whatever troubling time you are experiencing. You can read them in any order you please. Each is a separate reflection. Our faith is a wondrous resource in coping with life's unavoidable adversity. It is a bridge over troubled waters. Our firm belief is that our suffering is never in vain. We are taking up the cross of Christ and following his way to the resurrection.

I pray that during your troubling times you may maintain the attitude of St. Paul: "I consider the sufferings of the present to be as nothing compared to the glory to be revealed in us." (Romans 8: 18)

CHAPTER ONE

PRAYER IN TIMES OF TRIAL

"But let it be as you would have it, not as I."
—Jesus of Nazareth

We Catholics believe in the power of prayer. We take seriously what Jesus said, "Whatever you ask in my name I will give you."

My five year old granddaughter sincerely prayed one night, "Please, God, help the virus to go away so my dreams can come true because I want to save the world. With the virus, my Mom won't let me." She expresses her big dreams in prayer, which is so natural, beautiful, and innocent for the very young.

As we grow older, unfortunately, we often lose much of our innocence and optimism. The harshness and cruelty of life disillusions us. Many of us have given up praying because we no longer believe in a good and gracious God. We reason, "If God existed there would not be so much misery in the world." The world-wide pandemic validates their argument. An all-good God would not allow so much suffering. An all-powerful God would prevent it.

Nevertheless, many of us continue to pray and have faith. Our prayer sustains us, especially in times of adversity. During the pandemic, for example, we pray for the safety and good health of our loved ones. We ask God for a quick end to the pandemic. We beg for the return of a normal life with the security of our jobs and lifestyle. The list of our requests goes on. Our prayers come from the heart and reveal our concerns. As Jesus said, "Where your treasure is, there your heart is also." (Matthew 6: 21) We have faith in God and Jesus' promises, "Ask, and you will receive. Seek, and you will find. Knock, and it will be opened to you." (Matthew 7: 7)(1)

How do we pray during tough times? What does our prayer say about us, about the largeness of our hearts? Examining what Jesus teaches about prayer and the examples of Jesus and Mary in the Gospels can enlarge our perspective on prayer and how we approach God.

THE LORD'S PRAYER

In his Sermon on the Mount (Matthew 5-7), Jesus instructed his disciples on how to pray. He said, "Whenever you pray, go to your room, close your door, and pray to your Father in private. Then your Father who sees what no man sees, will repay you. In your prayer do not rattle on like the pagans. They think they will win a hearing by the sheer multiplication of words. Do not imitate them. Your Father knows what you need before you ask him." Jesus advocates praying alone in private, in solitude, in quiet. Prayer is not just saying the right words but in having the proper attitude. It is a stance of receptive listening in the stillness and trusting that God cares for us and already knows what we need. Prayer is not giving God information. It is letting Him shape us.

Jesus then gives a specific example of how to pray. He recommends we pray, "Our Father." We call upon God as a loving father. The word Jesus uses in his native Aramaic language is "Abba," which means father. It is a term of endearment, more accurately interpreted "Daddy." It was a scandal in Jesus' time to address God with such intimate familiarity. That is precisely how he wants his followers to address God.

The prayer proceeds, "Your kingdom come, your will be done." The focus is on letting God's will rule our lives. We build God's kingdom, not our own. We seek His will, not our own. Prayer, then, leads to a surrender to God establishing His reign in our lives.

Next, we make our requests. There are three. First, "Give us this day our daily bread," which is whatever we need to be true disciples of the Lord. Second, "And forgive us the wrong we have done as we forgive those who wrong us." We humbly and honestly admit our wrongdoing so we can sincerely ask for forgiveness. A bargain is struck with God. We implore God to forgive us on the condition that we forgive others. Without mercy toward others, we remain unforgiven by God. The final request, "Subject us not to the trial but deliver us from the evil one." As followers of Jesus, we expect suffering, trial, and adversity, and ask for deliverance. We pray to remain faithful and strong.

In the religion classes at the Catholic school I attended as a child, the sisters taught us about prayer. We learned the different purposes and forms of prayer with the acronym "ACTS," which signifies adoration, contrition, thanksgiving, and supplication. When we pray, we adore God and praise His goodness and graciousness. We express contrition, sorrow, for our sins and make a firm purpose of amendment to change our lives for the better. Aware that all we have comes from God, we thank Him for his many blessings. Finally, in supplication, we petition God to grant us more favors. However, we ask with this awareness, "Your heavenly Father knows all that you need. Seek first his kingship over you, his way of holiness, and all these things will be given you besides." (Matthew 6: 32-33) I would summarize these prayerful attitudes: Wow! Sorry! Thanks! Help! Of course, these various forms of prayer were exemplified by Jesus' life.

JESUS' PRAYER

The New Testament presents many glimpses of Jesus at prayer. He prayed frequently and regularly. He prayed at night, alone, in the desert, on the mountain. Even when the crowds were seeking him, he still went off alone to pray. He guarded his solitude with His Father. Before all the critical events in his life he spent extended time in prayer. It sustained his mission. He went off into the desert for 40 days to fast, pray, and be tempted before beginning his public ministry. He often invited his disciples to pray with him. Jesus was also a practicing Jew. As a child he was presented in the Temple, as the Jewish custom mandated. As an adult, he taught in the synagogues and made pilgrimages to the Jerusalem Temple for the high festivals.

We overhear Jesus' prayer in praise and thanksgiving, "I offer you praise, O Father, Lord of heaven and earth, because what you have hidden from the learned and the clever you have revealed to the merest children. Yes, Father, you have graciously willed it so. Everything has been given over to me by my Father." (Luke 10: 21-22). At the last supper, we hear Jesus appealing to his Father, "Father, the hour has come! Give glory to your Son that your Son may give glory to you." Then, he proceeds to request the protection of his disciples when he departs. He also prays "for those who will believe in me through their word. That all may be one as you, Father, are in me, and I in you; I pray that they may be one in us." (John 17: 1-26) Prayer brings about communion with God and one another. His last supper, which institutes for Christians the Eucharist, embodies all these forms of prayer within a community setting.

Jesus' most poignant prayer was on the night before and the day of his death. After his last supper, he asked his closest disciples to pray with him in the Garden of Olives. Three times he begged God that the cup of suffering and death be taken from him. Three times he ended the prayer in the same way, "But let it be as you would have it, not as I." His prayers of petition were always provisional. His desire was only to do his Father's will. Finally, on the cross as he was dying, he made one last prayerful request, not thinking of himself, "Father, forgive them; they do not know what they are doing." (Luke 23: 34)

His last words of prayer were for forgiveness, which is the essence of his message. The highest form of love is the love of our enemies, which requires forgiveness.

MARY'S PRAYER

Mary was Jesus' first and foremost disciple, present from the beginning and throughout his life to the foot of the cross. She is also a model of prayer. The Scriptures offer a few glimpses of Mary at prayer. When the Angel Gabriel announced she would be blessed to bear the Son of the Most High, Mary was confused and questioned how it could happen. Nevertheless, she assented, "I am the servant of the Lord. Let it be done to me as you say."

Mary could not contain the news. She went to visit her cousin Elizabeth and burst out with a prayer of praise and thanksgiving: "My being proclaims the greatness of the Lord, my spirit finds joy in God my savior. For he has looked upon his servant in her lowliness; all ages to come shall call me blessed. God who is mighty has done great things for me, holy is his name; His mercy is from age to age on those who fear him." (Luke 1: 26-56) Her prayer echoes the themes of the Lord's Prayer. She exclaims the greatness of God and her own humble lowliness. Her prayer reveals two essential attitudes: humility and a willingness to surrender to God's will with faith.

In John's Gospel (19: 25-27), Mary is silent at the foot of the cross. We can only imagine how this heart-broken woman prayed as she watched her son in the agony of dying. Undoubtedly, she prayed for the end of his sufferings. She did not understand the divine necessity of his death or the coming of his resurrection. However, because the Spirit of her son dwelt within her, she probably prayed as she did when the angel announced her pregnancy, "Your will be done." She may also have repeated the prayer of her son on the cross, "Father, forgive them; they do not know what they are doing." Even in this darkest moment she affirmed her confidence in the mercy, might, and greatness of God her savior.

OUR PRAYER

The prayerful attitudes of Jesus and Mary can sustain us during our dark times. Many do not pray because they do not believe in a loving God. However, perhaps they do not believe because they do not pray. In our materialistic society, we keep ourselves busy and distracted chasing a lifestyle. We make no time for solitude and prayer. The result is that we continue to live on the surface of life.

I believe that if we take the risk to enter into the solitude and truly listen, remarkable things can happen. We will sense the depth and mystery of life and our longings to be connected to that mystery. We will sense that we are part of something infinitely greater than ourselves. Wonder and awe at the simple feeling of being may emerge. The slowdown provides an invitation to take the time to be alone with ourselves and pray.

Most of us pray from time to time. Perhaps during our struggles to cope with the pandemic we pray more for health, safety, and the recovery of our lives. The prayers of Jesus and Mary suggest that we enlarge the scope of our praying to include praise, thanksgiving, and sorrow for our failings. Prayer is more than a mouthing of pious words. It reflects a changed heart. Prayer arises from our intimate communion with God that cannot be silenced. It is more about listening to God speaking than our talking. It is more about surrendering to God's will than letting Him know what we want. It is about receiving His blessings and finding a way to give back. Prayer enlarges our hearts and minds. Its fruits are a life lived with faith, hope, and charity.

What may be most challenging during our agonizing times is to pray, "Let it be." It is a prayer of surrender because we believe that God is with us working through this world-wide struggle. We do not understand how God's plan is unfolding through all the suffering, death, and loss. Yet, the words of St. Paul bolster us, "How deep are the riches and wisdom and knowledge of God! How inscrutable his judgments, how unsearchable his ways!" (Romans 11: 33) We believe that God's mercy will somehow bring new life out of the dying we experience. St. Paul wrote, "We know that God makes all things work together for the good of those who love him and who have been called according to his decree." (Romans 8: 28)

In fact, we may have an important role in making everything now work out for the good. Like Jesus and Mary, we ask, "What does God want of me now? What does this time of trial ask of me?" Our dedication to prayer will sustain and guide us. It will also inspire us to action for the benefit of all.

Hearing my granddaughter's prayer inspired me to write this article. I am reminded of Jesus' love of children. He said, "I assure you, unless you change and become like little children, you will not enter the kingdom of God." (Matthew 18: 3) Like a child's, our prayer must be filled with trust in the love of God who cares for us and knows our needs.

CHAPTER TWO

BEING CATHOLIC

"You must be made perfect as your heavenly Father is perfect."
—Jesus of Nazareth

We Catholics love Holy Mother Church, who is our comfort and guide.

I was born and raised Catholic. The Church has been my faith community from the beginning and still is. I'm proud to be Catholic. That does not mean that I have not been embarrassed and scandalized by the behavior of the hierarchy and my fellow Catholics. I have had my squabbles with the Church and left in anger and disappointment. But I always came back home. This is my family, warts and all, which I accept for better or worse.

One of the reasons I love being Catholic is because it espouses to be just that, "catholic." I learned in grade school that one of the essential marks of the Church was that it was catholic. The nuns explained that catholic means "universal." I never really liked that definition because it seemed so abstract and vague. It also suggested that the Church is the center around which all truth turns. That seemed arrogant to me.

I prefer the common dictionary definition of catholic as "including a wide variety of things, all-embracing." The Church is intended to be a mosaic of clashing colors that forms a beautiful picture. It is not a melting pot in which the flavors lose their individual tang to create an insipid broth. The Church is a mysterious unity in a wonderful diversity.

I believe that is how Jesus intended it to be. He called his disciples to be fishers of men and women, inviting them to cast their net into the sea to catch a boatload of various fish. He ate and drank with anyone who invited him to dinner, including the social outcasts. He instructed his apostles to preach the Good News to the ends of the earth. In obedience, after his death they began preaching throughout the known world. They believed they were making real the vision of the Book of Revelation "of a great multitude, which no one could count, from every nation, race, people, and tongue." (Revelation 7:9) All were gathered at the heavenly throne praising God. When I think of the Catholic Church, I say to myself, "Here comes everyone!"

The Church not only welcomes everyone in their uniqueness and diversity. It also tries to address all their spiritual needs in depth. Jesus instructed crowds about the kingdom of God, taught them how to pray, and healed the sick. Following his example, the disciples formed faith communities to address these needs. According to the Acts of the Apostles (2: 42, 4: 32), "They (Christians) devoted themselves to the apostles' instruction and the communal life, to the breaking of bread and the prayers....The community of believers were of one heart and one mind." Parishes today address these various spiritual needs by organizing commissions for Christian service, worship, and education. When I think of the Catholic Church, I say to myself, "Here everything human is welcome!"

As proud as I am about being Catholic, I am most aggrieved when the Church acts in less than catholic ways. A cursory reading of Church history reveals the many failures of the Church to be loving and all-embracing. We are both a saintly and sinful church, constantly in need of reform. Today I am saddened by how exclusive and divisive we Catholics can be. We judge one another by our own narrow standards. We proclaim ideals to which we often do not measure up. We consider ourselves bearers of the fullness of truth and close our minds to the wisdom of other religious traditions. We treat women as second-class citizens. We are preoccupied with sexual morality and abortion to the exclusion of other important moral issues. The list could go on. The hypocrisy scandalizes me. However, the bottom line is that I love my Church. I love it enough to stay and try to make us all better.

I believe I make the Church better by making myself a better Catholic. In recent years, I have tried to become more catholic, more all-embracing, by exposing myself to the wisdom of the Eastern spiritual traditions. Being catholic, I believe, means being open to the fullness of truth, wherever it may be found. I have been amazed at the wisdom and wealth of the Buddhist and Hindu traditions. The truths I have uncovered there compliment my Catholic faith and enrich my understanding of it. In opening my mind to diverse expressions of the one Truth we all seek, I have become a better Catholic.

THE SONG OF GOD

Let me give you an example. Recently, I have been reflecting on the *Bhagavad Gita (1)*, which expresses the essence of the Hindu faith. The name means "The Song of God." It portrays the battle between the forces of good and evil within our own psyches and the world at large. It also shows the paths to liberating victory. I view it as comparable to the Sermon on the Mount in our tradition, which summarizes the highest ideals of Jesus' teaching. The Sermon is the crown jewel of the Christian Scriptures. In the same way, the *Gita* is the diamond that reflects the bright light of the ancient Hindu scriptures, the Vedas and Upanishads. Hindus are particularly noted for their catholic outlook, their embracing of a diversity of spiritual insights, which the *Gita* highlights and harmonizes.

In particular, the *Gita* acknowledges that we all have different temperaments that influence how we approach God. The goal of all religions is union with God, which the Hindus call "Yoga." Each of us, however, must find our own path. There are no cookie-cutter guidebooks. Religious teaching can only point the way for us to discover the meaning for ourselves. The *Gita* identifies four different yogas, or paths, that correspond with our differing natural ways of seeking union with the Divine. Each has its own love language. These are the four paths:

<u>The Way of Action, Works, Service:</u>

Those of a practical nature, who want to make a difference in the world, follow this path. It is called "Karma Yoga." Those drawn to this way naturally perform acts of service for others. They are body-centered people, involved in the world. They prefer being active and want to see concrete results. They detest sitting around doing nothing. The *Gita* invites those who engage in the world to work with a selfless heart, not expecting a return, not being attached the outcomes. God is ultimately the Doer of all our actions, and we are His instruments. We offer our service as an act of worship to God. The *Gita* states: "Act for the action's sake. And do not be attached to inaction. Self-possessed, resolute, act without any thought of results, open to success or failure. This equanimity is yoga." (2: 47-48)

We Catholics believe in the power of active love. Authentic love is not just in words, but also in action. We are called to do, not just talk about, God's will in our lives. Watch the feet, not the lips. In our personal relationships, we perform acts of kindness and service. Gift-giving comes naturally. We learn about social justice issues, take a stand, and become actively involved. We promise never to be guilty bystanders. We of a practical temperament are drawn especially to Mark's Gospel which recounts so many stories of Jesus healing others. He is our example. We are not just to preach the Good News. We must also touches others' lives, heal the wounded and cast out the demons of the world.

The Way of Contemplation, Prayer:

Those who tend to be introspective and attuned to their inner life are drawn to this path. It is called "Raga Yoga." These individuals enjoy spending time alone with themselves and may be introverts. They want to get to know themselves at a deeper level. They are spirit-centered people who trust their intuitions. They believe that in knowing themselves they will know God. The *Gita* advises them to quiet their restless "wild monkey" minds and unruly emotions. Be still with themselves and know God. The *Gita* states: "Constantly mastering his mind, the man of yoga grows peaceful, attains supreme liberation, and vanishes into my bliss." (6: 15)

We Catholics believe in the power of prayer. Jesus taught us by his word and example to pray without ceasing. Imitating Jesus, we try to live our lives with a prayerful attitude, always aware of God's presence. We make time for prayer each day. We try to be intimate with ourselves, attuned to our thoughts, feelings, and reactions. We want to be authentic. In our relationships, we seek quality time together, not just incessant activity. We introspective people are fascinated by John's Gospel because it is the most contemplative one. That Gospel is an ongoing reflection on the mystery of the Word made flesh.

The Way of Knowledge, Wisdom:

Those who enjoy thinking about and analyzing things follow this way. This most challenging path is called "Jnana Yoga." These path-followers have a passion to know truth and hate deception. They are mind-centered people. They do not take matters at face value but look more deeply into them. They use the sword of discrimination, undistracted by unruly passions, to separate truth from lies, reality from illusion. The *Gita* instructs them to cultivate wisdom, use discrimination, and rejoice in the truth. The Mystery of God dwells within us. Through intimate, personal knowledge, we are united with Him. The *Gita* states: "Released from greed, fear, anger, absorbed in me and made pure by the practice of wisdom, many have attained my own state of being." (4: 10)

We Catholics believe that only truth will set us free. Jesus proclaimed that He is the Way, the Truth, and the Life. Our faith leads us to seek an ever-deeper awareness of the Divine Mystery in our lives. We are drawn to study the Scriptures and teachings of the Church to increase our knowledge. We witness to the truth in our interactions with others. In our relationships, we are careful to speak truthfully and express words of affirmation to those we love. We intellectually-minded are naturally attracted to Matthew's Gospel in which Jesus is portrayed as the Teacher of the new law, another Moses. The Gospel contains more direct words of Jesus than any other. It invites reflection on the words of the Master.

The Way of Devotion:

Those who are emotionally passionate individuals are drawn to this path. This most natural and popular way is called "Bhakti Yoga." The followers of this path are heart-centered people with an emotional temperament. They thrive on strong, loving relationships. They believe what Barbra Streisand sings, "People who need people are the luckiest people in the world." The *Gita* invites all to be devoted to God with their whole heart, mind, and soul. Give up attachments to any lesser desires and surrender completely to God. The way to bliss, lasting joy, is heartfelt devotion to God. The *Gita* states: "He who, devoted to me, is beyond joy and hatred, grief and desire, good and bad fortune—that man is the one I love best." (12:17)

We Catholics believe in the power of love. Jesus demonstrated his love for us by dying on the cross for us. He invites us to be devoted to Him and follow His example. We believe that love conquers all. Jesus healed the sick and cast out devils through the power of His divine love. The

Father's love raised Him from the dead. God is love. By loving God and one another we become God-like and united with Him. We seek an intimate personal relationship with Jesus and feel nourished by our devotional practices, such as the Eucharist, the rosary, and adoration before the Blessed Sacrament. We devotion-minded are drawn naturally to Luke's Gospel where Jesus is portrayed as a friend of sinners. Jesus shows mercy and compassion in His every encounter, and we seek to do the same.

THE BEATITUDES

The centerpiece of the jeweled necklace that is the Sermon on the Mount is the Beatitudes. My reflections on the *Gita* suggest a comparable set of Beatitudes:

> Blessed are they who perform their actions as worship, they shall be truly free.

> Blessed are they who renounce the fruits of actions, freedom will be theirs.

> Blessed are the lovers of silence, they shall have peace.

> Blessed are they who master their minds, they shall know bliss.

> Blessed are the open-minded, they shall find Truth.

> Blessed are they who hunger and thirst for Truth, wisdom shall be theirs.

> Blessed are the selfless, God's love shall fill their hearts.

Blessed are those with unwavering faith, they are God's beloved.

There is great joy in being Catholic, if we are really catholic in our outlook. Excluding others harms us. Ignoring the depth or our experience diminishes us. Closing our minds and hearts leads to division and misery. There is a great wealth of wisdom in our world and within ourselves if we only open our ears to hear it. Everyone and everything belongs. We can learn and grow in our interactions with everyone. The free exchange of ideas enriches us all and enables us to grow in intimacy. There is no greater joy than being catholic and united with the whole world. Such openness leads to union with God, the true goal of all religions.

CHAPTER THREE

MOTHER MARY

"I am the servant of the Lord. Let it be done to me as you say."
—Mary

We Catholics have a special devotion to Mary, the Mother of God. She is our model of devotion to her Son.

In troubled times we experience our lives as a battlefield. World leaders have declared war against the invisible enemy of COVID-19. However, we experience a deeper conflict with our own thoughts and feelings, our moods of anxiety and depression. We fight within ourselves. The enemy we see in the mirror is ourselves.

I'm noticing that in the most challenging periods of my life, my devotion to Mary increases. I look for the comfort of a nurturing mother.

As a psychologist, I have been meeting with my patients each day as they struggle against the invisible enemies of anxiety and depression. They look to me for comfort. At the end of the day, I return home tired, battle-weary. I relax by listening to music, which rarely fails to calm me. Recently, a Beatle song, "Let it be," caught my attention. Here are the words: "When I find myself in times of trouble, Mother/ Mary comes to me/ Speaking words of wisdom, 'Let it be.'/ And in my hour of darkness, she is standing right/ in front of me/ Speaking words of wisdom, 'Let it be.'"

These poetic words inspired reflections on a possible different approach during tough times like the pandemic. Instead of an aggressive masculine approach that tends to intensify conflicts, perhaps we can learn something important from the feminine wisdom expressed in that song. Mother Mary can be the role model for a complimentary path of healing and growth.

SURRENDERING

The title of the Beatle song reminds me of the words of Mary in Luke's Gospel (2: 26-56). The Angel Gabriel approached Mary, an unmarried, working-class, Jewish teenager, and announced that she would bear a child of great promise. Mary was troubled and confused because she had not been with a man. However, despite her questions and sense of inadequacy, she responded, "I am the servant of the Lord. Let it be done to me as you say." Mary surrendered and accepted the task. She gave up her desire for understanding and control and embraced the mystery that was about to unfold in her life. It would lead her down unknown paths. She demonstrated remarkable courage in surrendering to an open-ended future.

Mary was able to surrender with confidence because she believed that the pregnancy, despite the shame it would bring her as an unwed mother, was a blessing. When she met her pregnant cousin Elizabeth, she exclaimed, "My being proclaims the greatness of the Lord, my spirit finds joy in God my savior."

We experience the pandemic as a curse that we resist and fight against. We live with unbearable uncertainty as our normal lives are disrupted.

Our anxiety makes us imagine the worst. Perhaps, an attitude of courageous surrender may be more helpful in enduring the trials and losses yet to come. There may be a hidden blessing in this trial if we embrace it with confidence. What will we learn about ourselves? What strengths will we discover within ourselves? What does this pandemic ask of us?

For example, a middle-aged man related, "I hated the stay-at-home order. I always kept busy, working long hours and going out with friends. Then, it all stopped. I felt like a prisoner at home. I fought it for the longest time and complained bitterly. But at some point I relaxed with it. Surprisingly, I began to enjoy the slower life and time with my family and kids."

HEART-TREASURE

When the shepherds visited the newborn baby and related the angels' message, Mary listened with her heart. Luke relates, "Mary treasured all these things and reflected on them in her heart." As she watched Jesus "progress steadily in wisdom and age and grace before God and man," Mary observed carefully. Luke says, "His mother meanwhile kept all these things in memory" (Luke 2: 19, 51). Mary not only surrendered to the moment, she also contemplated what she experienced. She listened with her heart to discover its depth of meaning. She held the events in memory, meditating often on them. She sensed that something sacred was happening in these ordinary-appearing events. A child was born and grew up. However, she perceived something extraordinary. It is also noteworthy that she allowed the moments to enter her heart and not just her head, her rational mind.

Our masculine approach to problem –solving is to attack it with our rational minds and scientific tools. That promises to be effective combating the Coronavirus and providing effective medical treatment. However, this strategy is not so effective against the invisible enemies of fear and sadness. Mary's way of entering deeply into our experience and pondering it with our hearts is a more effective way of healing and growth through emotional turmoil. Like Mary, we search for the deeper meaning of our experience to set us free from our suffering and confusion. Her example invites us to meditate regularly on daily events to uncover the treasure of the present moment.

For example, a suburban woman reported, "Before the pandemic we had a very comfortable and secure life. Suddenly, both my husband and I lost our jobs. We worried constantly about paying our bills. Spending so much time alone at home, I began to reflect on the insanity of my worry and how important I had made our lifestyle. I'm beginning to ask myself what really matters to me, what really lasts. I appreciate the love of my husband and children much more now."

SORROWING

I have a special devotion to Our Lady of Sorrows. I attended a parish of that name for two years. When touring Rome, I frequently visited St. Peter's Basilica and spent considerable time meditating before Michelangelo's Pieta. I was moved by the sculpture of the youthful, heart-broken face of Mary holding her dead son. I admired Mary's courage and compassion.

In three of the Gospel accounts, all of the apostles fled after Jesus was arrested. They feared being killed by the Jews like their Master. Only Mary and some women remained to witness Jesus' death on the cross. In John's Gospel (19: 25-27), Mary, some women, and the beloved disciple stood before the cross. Jesus commanded Mary and the beloved disciple to care for each other. Mary demonstrated remarkable courage in the face of the suffering of her Son. The men ran away, while she stood her ground. She also showed a heart of tender compassion.

During the pandemic, the whole world is suffering terrible losses of life, lifestyle, and livelihood. We mourn these losses and fear what is yet to come. Our tendency may be to self-medicate the pain by denial, drugs, food, constant distraction, and so forth. We want to run away from it. Or we can follow the example of Mary and courageously open our hearts to experience the suffering of others and ourselves. Pain can close us up, making us hard-hearted and bitter, or the heart-break can open us to be compassionate. Mary's way leads us to embrace the suffering and become open-hearted. It is the path to authentic healing.

For example, a woman related, "Our mother was sick with COVID-19 and hospitalized. It was touch-and-go for a long time. We didn't think she would make it. The hardest part was that we could not be at her bedside. Our family pulled together, and we supported each other. This whole painful experience brought us closer."

REJOICING

After Jesus ascended, the apostles, Mary, and some women gathered in an upper room. I imagine that Mary had become the matriarch of the group and brought together her wounded children to heal. As mentioned above, in John's Gospel Jesus made Mary and the beloved disciple, who represents all the followers of Jesus, into a family. The compassionate mother would naturally want to help her children heal and find new life. She knew that healing could come only within a community of people who love and support one another.

As the sad, frightened group hid in that upper room, the unexpected happened. Suddenly, like a strong, driving wind and a burning fire, a divine Presence showed up. "All were filled with the Holy Spirit." Their sorrow turned to joy. Courage dispelled their fears. They began to speak boldly "about the marvels God has accomplished." The Spirit was one of energizing love, boundless joy, and courageous commitment to the truth of their experience of the risen Lord (Acts 2: 1-13).

We Americans pride ourselves as being rugged individuals, like the Lone Ranger, who can conquer any adversary. We believe that hard work and determination can accomplish great feats, but we have become dispirited. Troubled times, such as the pandemic, expose our vulnerability. With all of our technological prowess, we have not been able to eradicate the Coronavirus. However, Mary's gathering reveals a hidden strength at our disposal that far surpasses our individual efforts. It is the power of loving relationships. Our working together in love releases a force that can overcome any foe, especially the invisible enemies of hatred, loneliness, and fear.

For example, an anxious man confessed, "My anxiety has gone through the roof during the pandemic. I'm terrified of getting sick and dying. I would have fallen apart if I didn't have the love and support of my family. Staying home with them has been a blessing. I never realized how much I took them for granted and needed them."

My devotion to Mary sustains me during difficult times. I keep an icon of the Blue Madonna next to my man-cave chair. I often pray to her and meditate on her way: "Let it be." She embraces everyone and everything wholeheartedly, does not run away or try to control, and gathers all into one family. That will be the sure path to a renewed life.

CHAPTER FOUR

WORKS OF MERCY

"My religion is kindness."
—Dalai Lama

We Catholics are not loners. We have a strong sense of belonging to a faith community that reaches to the ends of the earth.

Many of us feel overwhelmed in this global war against COVID-19, not knowing what we need to do. Many have clear roles. Scientists work on improving vaccines. Health care workers treat the sick in clinics and hospitals. Politicians decide strategies for the common good, seeking a delicate balance between competing interests. But what is our role as ordinary citizens, foot soldiers in the trenches, in battling our invisible enemy? The uncertainty about what we can do increases our anxiety and sense of helplessness. What specifically does the pandemic ask of us individuals? What is the best way we can fight COVID-19 in our daily lives?

The Catholic faith in which I was raised and which still practice answers this compelling question. My faith has given me guidance throughout my life on how to live a full, flourishing life. Growing up, I attended our parish grade school which was run by the Sisters of St. Joseph. Every day, we had religion class which consisted of a review of the Baltimore Catechism. The Catechism contained the basic teachings of the Catholic faith in a question-and-answer format. For example, the question, "Why did God make you?" The answer, "To know, love, and serve Him and to be happy with Him in heaven." We had to memorize all the correct responses. The good nuns could be rigorous and demanding. They prepared us to meet the Bishop who would question us on the Catechism before receiving the sacrament of Confirmation. Sister said, "Don't you embarrass me!"

In the Catechism, we learned precisely what I believe in troubled times, such as the pandemic: to practice the corporal and spiritual works of mercy. This moral guidance comes from the Scriptures, mostly from the last judgment scene in Matthew 25: 31-46. The sheep are separated from the goats, based on their service to those in need. The judging king says, "I assure you, as often as you did it for one of my least brothers, you did it for me."

Mother Teresa, the saint of Calcutta, used the works of mercy as a guide for her life and her order of sisters. She said her religious order was not just a group of social workers. Their motivation was to serve the Lord. To demonstrate this, she held up five fingers, one at a time to match her words, and said, "You do this for me." She also believed we are all members of the Body of Christ today. She said, "We are His hands reaching out to the poor."

The works of mercy are not unique to Catholics or Christians. All the authentic religious traditions offer similar advice. The Dalai Lama best defined true religion when he said, "My religion is kindness." Faith, however, is not needed to appreciate this universal guidance to the good life. Anyone of good will, with open mind and heart, will come to the same conclusion about its value to our wellbeing. It is common sense. We need to practice what I learned as a child in a Catholic school.

The pandemic, as much as any world crisis, asks us all to practice the corporal and spiritual works of mercy. That is the path to health, resilience, and healing.

CARE FOR OTHERS

Let me explain these works of mercy, which are really as self-evident as the truth, "Treat others as you want to be treated." They offer practical, specific, concrete advice on how to live a meaningful and happy life. They do not merely promise a heavenly reward in the future; they show a path to our fulfillment in the present. We reap the benefits now. These activities also address the needs of the whole person—body, mind, and spirit. These practices can be done by anyone who is willing. It is the way of love in the here and now. "Bloom where you're planted," the popular saying advises. We can begin practicing works of mercy at home with our families and then perhaps, as we see fit and are able, extend ourselves outward to the community, nation, and world.

The corporal works of mercy address our material and physical needs:

- Feed the hungry.
- Give drink to the thirsty.
- Clothe the naked.
- Shelter the homeless.
- Visit the sick.
- Visit the imprisoned.
- Bury the dead.
- Give alms to the poor.

During the pandemic, for example, there are certainly many opportunities to engage in the corporal works of mercy. We begin taking care of the basic needs of our own families. In our society, many have lost their jobs, income, and financial security. Many need to be sheltered and fed. Soup kitchens have long lines. Homeless shelters are full. Unfortunately, we cannot visit the sick because of the danger of contagion. However, we can care for sick family members at home. We mourn the death of our loved ones and bury them with dignity, despite mandates against congregating. The ranks of the poor in our midst are swelling because of the economic slowdown. We seek ways of helping them survive. Each of us has a unique calling to serve in our own ways. It does not have to be great or dramatic, only done with a loving heart. There is abundant evidence that many are engaged in acting mercifully. These are silent heroes who need no applause.

For example, a young man who recovered from COVID-19, told me, "I was so sick I'm fortunate I survived. I want to donate my blood for antibodies to help others." A retired man said, "So many elderly are homebound. I volunteer as a driver to take them to doctor appointments. Many are starved for conversation." A woman with children related, "My elderly aunt has not been able to leave her house since the pandemic. I visit her regularly with the kids and visit from her porch. She is so appreciative." Another woman said, "I visit my sick and homebound family with cards and phone calls."

The spiritual works of mercy focus on our emotional, mental, and spiritual needs:

- Instruct the ignorant.
- Counsel the doubtful.
- Admonish the sinners.
- Comfort the afflicted.
- Forgive offenses willingly.
- Bear wrongs patiently.
- Pray for the living and the dead.

Again, during the pandemic, there are many opportunities to comfort, support, and forgive one another. We have suffered so many losses and need comforting. In this novel situation, uncertainty, confusion, and misinformation abound. Not only our children, but we adults also need education about the pandemic and clear answers to our questions about what to do to protect ourselves. These trying times bring out both the best and worst in all of us. Differing war strategies become politicized and contentious. Demonstrators protest police brutality and racial injustice. We need to speak our truth clearly and correct each other gently. To avoid divisiveness within our families and society, forgiveness is the antidote to the poison of anger. Amidst all the uncertainty and misguided turns we require patience to weather the storm. Through prayer, we experience our connection with all and affirm we are all in this together. Many bring each other emotional and spiritual support behind the scenes to maintain hope.

For example, a man who loves to surf the Internet related, "I look for informative articles about the pandemic and send them to family and friends. I believe knowing the facts can help overcome anxiety." A young woman said, "Since I cannot go to the gym, I go for walks every day. Whenever I pass people, I make a point of greeting them cheerfully. There's too much gloom around." Another woman told me, "I refuse to engage in any conversations that bash President Trump, politicians, policemen, and protesters. I hate the divisiveness and negativity which only brings us all down." One considerate husband confided in me, "My wife's going crazy with worry about being infected. I'm much calmer about it, but I stay home and take extra precautions when I have to go out to ease her worry."

SELF-CARE

What we do for others also benefits us. We show mercy to others as "another self" who reflects us. In helping others, we help ourselves. Our acts of kindness make us feel happy, fulfilled, and connected. Our isolation is overcome. These practices also remind us of our own vulnerability that requires our attention.

For example, a patient of mine was hospitalized by the Coronavirus. He was grateful for the care he received by the medical staff that he believed saved his life. He said, "I was so sick I nearly died. During the quarantine I gained weight. I neglected myself and paid the price. I ate and drank more just to cope. I was irritable and took it out on the family. Now I feel so guilty. This has been a wakeup call for me to take a serious look at how I live."

We need to care for ourselves as much as we have compassion for others to maintain our health and wellbeing. Alcoholics Anonymous, that wise and practical program of recovery, teaches the importance of self-care to avoid relapse into addiction and mental illness. The program uses the acronym "HALT" which means: "Don't be hungry, angry, lonely, or tired." We have to care for the whole person, body, mind, and spirit, to stay on the path of healing and growth. In other words, self-care demands that we apply the corporal and spiritual works of mercy to ourselves.

Mercy, kindness, and compassion are meant to be shared, mutual. By practicing these virtues, we develop nurturing relationships with partners, family, and friends who in turn care for us. A Chinese proverb states, "Life is an echo. What you send out comes back." The echo of our good deeds reverberates around the world.

Experts underline the importance of total self-care. They demonstrate that the body, mind, and spirit are intimately connected. We are rational animals, embodied spirits. Neglect of any part will affect the whole. To maintain a strong immunity system to fight off COVID-19, we have to have healthy bodies. To keep our bodies healthy requires a wholesome lifestyle and the avoidance of stress. To avoid stress, we must live a meaningful and satisfying life, caring for others. Giving in to despair will only make us susceptible to physical, emotional, and spiritual illness. Nurturing our bodies, minds, and spirits requires courage and builds resilience.

Mercy makes us resilient. It is the powerful weapon we all carry in this war. We are all essential workers. Our acts of kindness, however small, possess a great, lasting significance. The pandemic currently engulfs the whole world. Our earth will defeat the Coronavirus invasion and heal through our acts of compassion. Beginning with ourselves, we extend kindness and mercy throughout all our relationships to the ends of the earth.

CHAPTER FIVE

SMALL ACTS OF KINDNESS

*"It isn't necessary to great things,
but rather small things with great love."*
—Mother Teresa

We Catholics believe in the power of love. God is love. If we live in love, we live in Him and He dwells in us. Loving God and our neighbor fulfills all the commandments.

As reported previously, my five-year-old granddaughter sincerely prayed one night, "Please, God, help the virus to go away so my dreams can come true because I want to save the world. With the virus, my Mom won't let me." She has big dreams, which is so natural, beautiful, and innocent for the very young.

However, we adults often lose our idealism and innocence as we face crises, such as the pandemic. Our temptation is in the opposite direction of thinking big. We tend to become disheartened in the face of the intense opposition and give up. "There's nothing I can do," we tell ourselves. In the case of the pandemic, we longed for science to rescue us with a magical cure-all vaccine, but many refuse to be vaccinated. Meanwhile, a sense of helplessness may rule our lives.

In my daily work as a psychologist, my patients tell me of their distress during trying times and their efforts to cope. They mirror the struggles of our society. We wonder how this difficulty can become an opportunity for healing and growth.

OUR SMALLNESS

We feel powerless, small, and insignificant, for example, in the face of the magnitude of the pandemic. A microscopic virus, like an alien invader, has taken over the entire planet. With all our efforts, we have not been able to stop completely the advance of this plague, even with the availability of vaccines. Daily we view images from around the world of sickness and death. We listen to the news each night to hear the numbers of infections, hospitalizations, and deaths. Economies struggle to recover.

We Americans also feel humbled and humiliated. We took pride in being the greatest nation on the earth. We are a people of great expectations. However, despite our immense resources, scientific expertise, and advanced health care, we are suffering a disproportionately larger number of infections and deaths than the rest of the world. Ironically, as people of color suffer more in our country, we suffer more than the poorer nations of the world. How could we be so unprepared? Our sense of humiliated helplessness has been transformed into rage that looks for scapegoats. Various political groups fight each other instead of attacking COVID-19 with a united front. We throw blame around. We hide our smallness behind a mask of aggressiveness.

We instinctively view the pandemic from the dark cave of fear, which makes us feel small and helpless. Anxiety, anger, and angst come from the same root word that means "constricting, narrowing." We see ourselves as alone, separate, and shrunken in this war against a seeming insurmountable enemy. Our lives are reduced to a fight for survival for our health, livelihood, and lifestyle. In our fear, we see only darkness. We imagine the worst and a grim future.

PART OF A LARGER WHOLE

It bears repeating that the word *catholic* means universal. Our Catholic faith invites us to see things from a larger, more universal, perspective.

Living in fear's dark cave we see no way out. However, we can escape that mental cave and enlarge our view and hope for a new life. We can ascend to the mountaintop of our wise mind and gain a panoramic view of our situation. From there, we see that everything belongs, nothing is left out. It is a view from the perspective of love, which is all-embracing. We see that we are part of a larger whole and can make an essential contribution to the wellbeing of the whole. We are all interconnected. The largeness of the universe resides in each of us. We are not separate, isolated individuals fighting for survival. Our focus needs to be not just on surviving but rather on flourishing and creating a new earth from the tragedy of the pandemic.

This magnificent vision is expressed by many diverse voices. For example, Christians proclaim that Jesus the Christ is the Alpha and Omega, the beginning and the end. The whole universe and all its parts, including us, come from Him and will return to Him. "It pleased God to make absolute fullness reside in him and by means of him to reconcile everything in his person, both on earth and in heaven, making peace through the blood of his cross." (Colossians 2: 19-20). We groan under the weight of the pandemic for redemption. In fact, Paul adds, that our cries are joined with the longings of all creation for freedom. "Yes, we know that all creation groans and is in agony even until now. Not only that, but we ourselves, although we have the Spirit as first fruits, groan inwardly while we await the redemption of our bodies." (Romans 8: 22-23)

Paul offers another image of our unity and connectedness. We are all members of the body of Christ: "The body is one and has many members, but all the members, many though they are, are one body; and so it is with Christ....If one member suffers, all the members suffer with it; if one member is honored, all the members share its joy." (I Corinthians 13: 12, 26)

The Eastern traditions suggest a similar vision of wholeness and interdependence. The entire universe is like a vast, limitless net of the god Indra. On each of the nodes of the net is a precious jewel. Each jewel reflects the brilliance of one another and the whole bespectacled, far-reaching net. We are those priceless jewels, linked to all others.

Some scientists today propose a third image of wholeness, called the Gaia hypothesis. In Greek mythology, Gaia was the goddess who personified the earth. According to this hypothesis, living organisms interact with their inorganic surroundings on earth to form a self-regulating, complex system, a web of life. All the parts of this system work together in a delicate balance to maintain the proper conditions for life on earth. Our task as humans is to become attuned to the natural rhythms of our universe in which we are a part. The life of the universe runs through our veins. The poet Dylan Thomas wrote, "The force that through the green fuse drives the flower/Drives my green age."

As parts of the larger whole, we are all essential workers. During the initial shutdown, certain groups, such as health care, grocery, sanitation workers, were considered essential. In reality, we all perform indispensable functions in the war against the Coronavirus. Victory will depend on each of us fulfilling our unique roles.

THE 36 CLUB

There is a legend in Jewish lore about the fundamental importance of our good works, however trivial they may seem to us. I heard this story at a workshop given by Rabbi Rami Shapiro. The whole world keeps from falling apart because at any one time 36 people are embraced by the Divine Feminine. That is, they perform acts of compassion. Why the number 36? The number is symbolic. Six times six equals 36, which signify all creation. Two times 18 equals 36. That is the number of individuals who live two lives, one for others and the other for themselves. At any moment it is not the same 36 people performing good acts to keep the earth afloat. At any given moment, anyone can be awake and be a blessing to someone. Our kindness at any moment may be the decisive act that keeps our world going.

POWER OF SMALLNESS

It is often the little ones who have the greatest impact on our world, rather than the rich, famous, and powerful. Jesus exemplifies the power of smallness. The Son of God was born in a stable, in poverty. He grew up in a working-class neighborhood in Nazareth. He spent His whole life, about 30 years, in a tiny Roman-occupied country on the eastern end of the Mediterranean. He never left that country or travelled more than a hundred miles. His public life of preaching and healing lasted less than three years, and He was executed as a common criminal. As unremarkable as His life was from the outside, he saved the world.

Jesus encouraged His followers to value the little way. He taught them the beatitudes, which affirm the blessedness of the poor in spirit, the sorrowing, the lowly, and the persecuted. He spoke in parables which underlined the enormous significance of good works. He compared His Spirit-filled disciples to mustard seeds, the smallest seed that produces one of the largest plants. They were also like leaven that causes the whole mass of dough to rise. Jesus explained his parable of the seed which falls on different ground as various people who hear His message. He said, "But what was sown on good soil is the man who hears the message and takes it in. He it is who bears a yield of a hundred-or-sixty- or thirtyfold." (Matthew 13: 1-43)

Marcus Aurelius, the philosopher-Caesar, who lived a century after Jesus, expressed a similar wisdom. Ironically, he mistrusted the Christian sect but shared many of their insights. He saw the world as one unified, sacred body: "Everything is interwoven, and the web is holy; none of its parts are unconnected. They are composed harmoniously, and together they compose the world. One world, made of all things. One divinity, present in them all." (1) He also encouraged all to recognize their inner power and take full responsibility for their task to make the world a better place. "It's time you realized you have something in you more powerful and miraculous than the things that affect you and make you dance like a puppet." (12: 19) In Christian terms, that something is the indwelling Spirit which is the source of our power.

Mother Teresa, the sainted nun who served the poorest of the poor, demonstrated the power of small acts of kindness. She gave the dying destitute on the streets of Calcutta a place to die with dignity. She cared for one person at a time. Her words can never be reiterated too often: "It isn't necessary to do great things but rather to do small things with great love."

During the pandemic and other stressful times, we can make a real difference by our small acts of kindness. Instead of cursing the darkness in fear, we can light a candle of love. Jesus said, "You are the light of the world...your light must shine before men so that they may see goodness in your acts and give praise to your heavenly Father." (Matthew 5: 14, 16) We can choose to show up as our best self in these trying times. No action is insignificant if it is done with a heart of love. The power of our love will transform the world. There is abundant evidence that many of us are making a noticeable difference by our good deeds. Here is a selection of what I hear on a daily basis in sessions:

"I'm in a funk and can't concentrate on my work. I'm fortunate to have a job and will push on regardless."

"When I have a panic attack, I just breathe deeply, smile, and remind myself it's a wonderful world."

"I feel so overwhelmed working from home and caring for the kids. I feel like running away, but I don't."

"I hate wearing a mask. I do it out of consideration for others."

"I refuse to bash President Trump, the politicians, the police, or the protesters. There's already too much negativity."

"I want to escape my worries by drinking. I stop myself because I know what it will do to my family and to me."

"My wife obsesses about the family becoming infected. It gets on my nerves, but I listen and try to reassure her."

"I spent so much time alone during the stay-at-home order. I prayed for the safety of my family and the whole world. I'm praying more now than ever."

"Since the shutdown, I have spent a lot of time outdoors. I decided to volunteer to clean up our local park."

"I have been so moody since being laid-off. I'm making every effort to lift my spirits and not bring down my family. I try to keep a friendly attitude with everyone I meet."

"We take groceries to our grandparents and have a porch visit every week."

"I refuse to give in to discouragement. I want to help keep m,y family strong and positive."

During crises such as the pandemic, we do not have to take on the burden of rescuing the world nor give up in hopelessness. Each of us has an important role in healing our world by showing up as our best self. We have special gifts of time, talents, and treasures that we can share with others. My gift is to write and sit with my patients. We are all part of a larger whole with an inner power that inspires us to give of ourselves. It is the power of love and compassion. By our small acts of kindness together we will create a new and better world.

CHAPTER SIX

GOD'S TEMPERAMENT

"Everything that is has its being through the love of God."
—Julian of Norwich

We Catholics believe in the communion of saints. The community of believers extends to the past, present, and future. We can draw from the strength and insight of many who lived exemplary lives.

In therapy, my patients and I work together to make sense of their painful experiences. As many in the past have done, we may turn to religion for understanding. In the 1980s, Jerry Falwell, the founder of the Moral Majority, called the HIV/AIDS pandemic God's punishment for the sin of homosexuals and the society that tolerates them. The popular evangelists, Billy Graham and Pat Robertson, echoed this message. They likened it to the plague of locusts God inflicted on the Egyptians for holding the Israelites captive.

Today, many see the pandemic as one of the signs of Armageddon, the final battle between good and evil in the Book of Revelation. God announced that before the second coming of Christ Four Horsemen would ravage the earth. One of those Horsemen is several plagues of God's wrath to punish idol-worshipers. The other Horsemen, representing violence, war, and famine have also made their appearance in the view of many religious-minded.

God's wrath is also seen in His permitting the forces of evil to run rampant in the world. Some see the pandemic as the work of the devil. The invisible enemy of the Coronavirus is attributed to a powerful hidden force and given a face. The face of the devil is seen in society's misfits, those held morally responsible for the calamity.

Throughout the history of pandemics, interpreting it in religious terms as the wrath of God or the work of the devil has led to persecutions. (1) In an effort to seek reconciliation with God and defeat Satan, groups rose up to rid society of undesirables, those sinners viewed as provoking God's displeasure. These sinners became scapegoats sacrificed to a vengeful God.

For example, Jews were banned or killed not only for killing Jesus but also for a conspiracy to annihilate Christianity with the plague. To placate God's wrath, sinners were identified and cast out: prostitutes, religious dissenters, foreigners, and witches. The undesirables were hunted down, beaten, and often killed. Such persecutions were a medieval version of contemporary ethnic cleansing.

CONSPIRACY THEORIES

It appears that the apocalyptic battleground has shifted to the political arena today, to the dismay of many of us. The war has shifted from the common enemy, COVID-19, to battles between political adversaries. Some called the 2020 election "the most important election in the history of our country." It was portrayed as a choice between good and evil. Democrats and Republicans both accused each other of deceit and power-grabbing. The shadow of the end times darkened the political skies.

Conspiracy theories fuel the intensity of these battles. While most Americans take these theories with a grain of salt, some claim that hidden, powerful forces operate behind the scenes, orchestrating the political drama. For example, one man wrote me a text, "The real scary thing is the people pulling puppet strings. The Democratic Party has been taken over by some real frightening people." Democrats also imagine conspiracies. Some called President Trump a "Demagogue" who wants to be a Fascist dictator, implying he was the anti-Christ. They see a hidden plot to destroy democracy.

A fearful paranoid attitude spawns these conspiracy theories. The word paranoia comes from the Greek words *para* (besides) and *nous* (thought, mind). It is a parallel, alternative view of reality. The world is experienced as hostile and threatening. Enemies hide everywhere, like bogie men under the bed. Those who embrace these theories divide the world into two neat groups: winners and losers, righteous and sinners, the good and the evil. Of course, they see themselves on the side of winning, righteousness, and goodness. They consider themselves "true believers," while others are naïve and ignorant.

Ironically, these believers hold a blind faith in their chosen authorities without relying on evidence or logic. Their conclusions are drawn from questionable facts, rumors, and outright lies gleaned from Internet sites. The conspiracy hunters internalize the wrathful God in whom they put their faith and seek to appease Him through vengeful sacrifice. Their mission is to save the world by eradicating the immoral, who are demonized. Consequently, they hunt for scapegoats, who may have various faces: the Chinese, the LGBT community, the radical socialist left, white supremacists, unruly blacks, brutal police, anarchists, the political opposition, President Trump, and so forth.

These conspiracy theories are really an attempt to self-medicate fear. From the dark cave of fear, we identify with groups and fixed ideas for safety. We cannot tolerate the lack of certainty, clarity, and control we experience during the pandemic and are angry about it. We divide the world into good and evil and stand on the side of righteousness. To fight the invisible enemy of the plague and our own fear, we give the enemy a face which we seek to conquer. A visible common enemy is easier to grapple with.

The contentiousness, however, masks our fear, our sense of helplessness. Joining a protesting group gives us a sense of solidarity and strength in our weakness. The absolute rightness of the cause compensates for our insecurity and uncertainty. Possessing a secret truth makes us feel special. The approval of the group bolsters our low self-esteem. From a religious perspective, we feel noble believing God is on our side in the war against evil-doers.

WHO IS YOUR GOD?

Battling each other in the name of a wrathful God will never bring peace. It will only escalate into more hostility, division, and violence. God, of course, does not change, but our understanding of Him does. However, there are other ways to view God that can foster a more promising approach to the pandemic.

The notion of an angry, judgmental God governs the thinking and behavior of many Christians. Research indicates that 92% of Americans believe in God, but in four different Gods. Their views of God's character differ radically. Thirty one percent believe in an Authoritarian God, a wrathful, sin-hating deity. Sixteen percent put their trust in a Critical God, who brings justice and will make everything right in the end. Another quarter (24%) believes in a Distant God, the cosmic creative force within and beyond the universe. Finally, only 23% put their faith in a Benevolent God, the forgiving friend of sinners, who cares for us and brings peace. (2)

We believe we are "made in the image and likeness of God." Our view of God is not inconsequential. It affects how we view ourselves as humans who reflect His presence in the world. If we seek to be more God-like in our behavior, our image of God takes on a critical importance. How we view God and ourselves shapes our behavior.

JULIAN OF NORWICH: NO WRATH IN GOD

To make sense of the pandemic, there is another way to understand how God is working, other than as an authoritarian, wrathful, critical God. Dame Julian of Norwich, a 14th century mystic, had visions of an all-loving God which she recorded in her *Revelations of Divine Love (3)*. She nearly died from a serious illness and lived through the Black Death in voluntary seclusion as a hermit in medieval England. Nearly half the population died during that pandemic, yet she maintained a hopeful attitude.

She wrote: "During all my showings it was revealed to me again and again that our beloved God cannot forgive, because he cannot be angry....It is vital for us to believe that the One who dissolves and destroys our wrath and makes us humble and gentle is himself clothed in that same gentle and humble love, which is the opposite of wrath. I saw in truth that wherever our Beloved appears, peace is restored and anger has no place. I did not see any kind of anger in God—neither in passing nor for an extended period of time. The truth, as I perceive it, is that if he were to be even one iota angry, we would have no life, no place to be, no being....While we may feel anger, disagreement, and strife within ourselves, we are always mercifully enfolded in the Beloved's gentleness, kindness, and humble accessibility." (Chapter 49)

Julian of Norwich had sixteen visions, which she called showings, of God's love. In this showing, she experienced the absence of God's wrath and the extent of His love. Her optimism was remarkable in a time of the horrific Black Plague that killed off nearly half the population of Europe. Unlike many in the Christian culture of her time, she did not interpret the plague as the punishment of an angry God for our sins nor as the work of the devil.

Instead, Julian only had visions of God's love for the world, which she came to understand as the loving presence of the Lord in her life. She affirmed repeatedly that God does not punish us, but loves us graciously and irresistibly into new life. She wrote: "Then he showed me a small thing, the size of a hazelnut, nestled in the palm of my hand. It was round as a ball. I looked at it with the eyes of my understanding and thought, 'What can this be?' And the answer came to me: 'It is all that is created.' I was amazed that it could continue to exist. It seemed to me to be so little that it was on the verge of dissolving into nothingness. And then these words entered my understanding: 'It lasts, and will last forever, because God loves it. Everything that is has its being through the love of God.'" (Chapter 5)

Further, she saw God's love and wisdom guiding everything. She wrote: "Next, I saw God in a single point in my mind. I contemplated his point with my full attention and realized that God is the center of all that is and the Doer of all that is done....For I saw truly that God is responsible for everything, no matter how little, and nothing happens by luck or chance. Everything is guided by the all-seeing wisdom of God. If we view things as happening by accident, it is because we lack divine sight. In God's all-seeing wisdom, all things have their rightful place since before the beginning of time. He brings everything, always, to its perfect conclusion." (Chapter 11)

Julian perceived a divine conspiracy, even in the horror of the Black Plague. The power of God's love and wisdom was working mysteriously behind the scenes. All would unfold according to His will and come to a perfect conclusion. The power of evil and sin were considered as nothing in comparison with God's omnipotent love. She wrote: "I believe that sin has no substance, not a particle of being, and cannot be detected at all except by the pain it causes. It is only the pain that has substance for a while, and it serves to purify us and make us know ourselves and ask for mercy....What this means is, 'It is true that sin causes all this pain, but all will be well, and all will be well, and every kind of thing will be well.'" (Chapter27) Love conquers all. In the end, we will be victorious over suffering and death. We only have to cooperate with God's grace.

Even suffering has a benefit now. Julian wrote as she gazed upon a crucifix while critically ill: "And then our Beloved cheerfully suggested to my mind, 'Is there any point to your pain or your grief, now?' And I found that I was completely happy. I realized that what Christ meant to show me is that we are hanging on the cross with him right now—in our pain, in our suffering, even in our dying—and that if we willingly stay with him, he will, by his grace, convert all our distress into delight." (Chapter 21) Julian did not minimize all the suffering the Black Plague caused. However, she was confident that God's love, revealed on the cross, would transform it into joy.

Such a hopeful vision of God and His love for us and the world can transform the way we work through the pandemic. However, faith in such a vision can only be cultivated in prayer. The need for developing a more Christ-like mind and heart is especially essential in times of tribulation like these. Nevertheless, the folly of the cross scandalizes still today and requires faith to accept it.

A DIVINE CONSPIRACY

Julian received the revelation of a divine conspiracy of love, not hatred. The word *conspiracy* comes from the Latin words *cum* (with, together) and *spirare* (to breathe). We breathe together with God, sharing His breath who is the Holy Spirit. God's Spirit enlivens us. What a grand vision! How are we to breathe together with the God of love during the pandemic? Some attitudes are suggested:

Compassion

We are all suffering together during the pandemic. No one is excluded. When we fight against and blame each other, we forget this plain fact. We mourn many losses to ourselves and our loved ones: of health, financial security, and comfortable lifestyle. Countless have died without family presence. We are also in the grip of anxiety about how much more we will lose. There is no clear end in sight. We need to see beyond our hostile reactions and have compassion for ourselves and those around us. The word *compassion* comes from the Latin words *cum* (with, together) and *passio* (suffering). We are suffering together, and Christ is suffering with us.

A middle-age woman came to see me because she was having panic attacks during the pandemic. She never saw herself as an anxious person until now. Her whole life she distracted herself from her anxiety by keeping busy. She confessed, "I used to hate my older sister because she was so bossy and controlling. I never realized that she was struggling with anxiety like me. Now I have compassion for her." She could not see another's fear until she admitted her own.

Humility

In the grip of anxiety, we cannot tolerate uncertainty or the loss of control. We want guarantees of safety and security. Our secret desire is to be all-knowing and all-powerful to avoid all dangers. We want to play God. Of course, we know that is unrealistic. So, we may attempt to be masters of our own small universe by identifying with special groups, noble causes, and fixed ideas. We imagine we have all the answers, while others are ignorant. Our mission is to rescue others with our certain truths. We become God-like judges, blaming others. However, when we believe we alone possess the truth, there is no dialogue or mutual learning. Discussions often degenerate into hostile confrontations. What is needed is a sense of humility that the truth is larger than ourselves. It is our task to search out its meaning together.

A retired patient of mine had a domineering father who punished him for any disagreement. He grew up angry and resentful of anyone in authority. In our working together he learned to listen to himself and others with an open mind. He said, "I used to avoid talking about religion and politics because that always led to fights. Now, I welcome these discussions and don't become threatened. We are just sharing opinions. I want to learn from those who have a different point of view. I value relationships more than being right."

A woman told me, "I stopped watching the news because it is all so negative and makes me more anxious. I blamed the fake news for creating drama but then realized how much I both hated and loved it. Something drew me to the drama." We talked about how the news covers what draws an audience. The news reflects our culture which is fascinated by all the conflicts reported. It is as if we are watching gladiator games with a secret blood lust, waiting to see the last person standing.

Patience

We Americans are fighters. That is our strength and our weakness. We set high goals for ourselves, work hard to overcome obstacles, and refuse to give up. But we struggle to accept limits. The President declared war against the Coronavirus. We took up arms in the war but have become impatient with the lack of progress in defeating this invisible enemy. The battleground has shifted to a political fight over war strategies. Again, we are deadlocked.

Victor Frankl, the Holocaust survivor, famously said, "When we are no longer able to change a situation, we are challenged to change ourselves." Now the field of battle needs yet again to shift to ourselves. We are invited to discover a peaceful and healing attitude within ourselves. We need a patience that will come only from discovering a meaning in our suffering. Julian of Norwich endured great suffering through her belief that her sufferings were united with those of Christ, who would transform them into joy.

An elderly woman told me, "The stay-at-home order did not change my life. I'm old and sickly, so I stay home anyway. I watch all the suffering on TV and pray for my family, our country, and the world. I ask God to help us get through this. I also offer up my suffering from all my medical problems."

Hope

Fear naturally alerts us to danger. However, when it becomes excessive as in these uncertain times, we tend to exaggerate the threats. We see danger lurking in the background and develop conspiracy theories to protect ourselves. Being preoccupied with hidden, powerful enemies only leads to intense conflict and despair.

In contrast, Julian of Norwich suggested another kind of conspiracy rooted in love. She saw signs of God's love and wisdom operating everywhere, even during the Black Plague. So she could proclaim with confidence, "All will be well, and all will be well, and every kind of thing will be well." We need such an attitude shift to acknowledging the power of love. We need to have confidence in our resourcefulness and resilience to overcome adversity. Having compassion, humility, and patience during these trying times will unleash the power of love. The conspiracy of love, in turn, will sustain our hope.

During the pandemic and other stressful times, conspiracy theories abound. We can breathe together the poison of hatred or the elixir of love. The optimistic vision of Dame Julian of Norwich can offset our fearful tendency towards a hateful defensiveness. She acknowledges the infinite power of God's love over hate. She wrote, "While we may feel anger, disagreement, and strife within ourselves, we are always mercifully enfolded in the Beloved's gentleness, kindness, and humble accessibility." The divine conspiracy of love will enable us to prevail over the pandemic and our fears.

CHAPTER SEVEN

A VISIONARY FOR OUR TIMES

"He wants us to realize we never suffer alone, but always together with him."
—Julian of Norwich

We Catholics value tradition which shapes who we are. It is a treasure house that enriches our current thinking.

As a psychologist, I talk daily with patients who have struggled to keep from falling into the pit of discouragement as the pandemic has unfolded. They mourn the losses of health, lifestyle, and livelihood with no clear end in sight. Dread and uncertainty hold them hostage. They fear being overwhelmed by an accumulation of more yet unknown losses." Who can guide us through this calamity?" they ask.

As unprecedented as this pandemic seems, history reveals the regular occurrence of deadly epidemics. The worst, of course, was the Black Plague that began in the Middle Ages and has lasted in some form and some places to the present day.

One figure stands out as a guide through that plague and possible patron saint of pandemics, the aforementioned Dame Julian of Norwich. Little is known of her personally. She lived in seclusion through three waves of the Black Plague in Norwich, England, where it claimed nearly half the population as victims. Death was everywhere. At times, there were not enough survivors to bury the mounting corpses. The plague also provoked political upheaval, class conflict, and hostility, which today's pandemic echoes. Peasants revolted against their royal masters; many were killed or executed. Julian wrote about her experience from a faith-filled perspective in a classic text entitled *Revelations of Divine Love* (1). She was the first woman to write in English, like Chaucer, in the 14th century.

Julian (her real name is unknown) herself experienced a near-death illness. She wrote: "When I was 30 years old, God sent me that illness I had asked for in my youth. For three days and three nights I lay in my bed, and on the fourth night I was given the last rites of the Holy Church. No one expected me to live through the night, yet I lingered for another two days. I kept thinking I was about to die, and everyone who sat with me thought so too. I was still young enough to be sad about dying." (Chapter 3)

She miraculously recovered and received 16 visions which she recorded in her writing. She faced numerous deaths of loved ones throughout her life and almost died herself. Yet, she never lost hope, frequently exclaiming, "All will be well, and all will be well, and every kind of thing shall be well." What is the secret of her hope that can guide us through our pandemic trial by fire?

PANDEMIC PAIN

The pandemic is doubly dangerous. The Coronavirus robs us of life, while the fear virus kills our spirit. We mourn losses to our health and normal way of life. We live in the grip of uncertainty, begging for the return of the familiar. For example, Jennifer, the mother of three children, told me, "I'm frustrated and exhausted. I go to work early every morning and return at noon to supervise my children's online learning. My husband works from home and takes care of the kids in the morning. I'm worried that our children will be so far behind educationally that they will never recover. When will this thing end?"

Jennifer is not alone. Surveys indicate that nearly a third of Americans are suffering from clinical levels of anxiety and depression. Experts project the emotional aftermath of the pandemic will last at least a decade. We are being traumatized. We try to cope the best way we can, without the benefit of a guidebook. In my practice, I observe three responses to the overpowering emotions provoked by the pandemic: denial, indulgence, and distraction.

Many people refuse to believe the seriousness of the pandemic. They live in denial and call it a "hoax" or a "plandemic." Some believe it is a conspiracy caused by the Chinese to remove President Trump and promoted by the Democrats to discredit him. They think the numbers of sick and dead are exaggerated. They say, "COVID is much less deadly than other illnesses like cancer and heart disease, which do not warrant a shutdown of our economy." Others frankly minimize the danger. For example, some of the young people who return to college gather for parties. They say, "COVID is no big deal. We may get sick, but we are young and healthy. We will recover quickly." Still others suffer from "pandemic fatigue." They are exhausted adjusting to the disruption of their lives, are preoccupied with it ending, and are numb to the mounting numbers of casualties.

A second group feels overwhelmed by a fear of getting sick and dying. They live restricted lives to feel safe. For example, a 50-year-old woman with diabetes and high blood pressure reported, "I'm terrified of being infected. COVID would kill me with my conditions. So, I stay at home and don't leave. I watch my husband's activities so he keeps safe. I won't let the children or grandchildren come into the house until this is all over." She is living in physical, emotional, and social shutdown for protection. She has become a prisoner of fear and a warden of others.

A third group distracts themselves from the threat of the pandemic. They keep busy, avoid talking about the dangers, and do not even think about it. For example, one man told me, "I keep myself busy with work and don't even think about the pandemic. I don't watch the news. I used to go to the bar to forget about things. Now I just drink at home." The national version of distracted living is all the attention given to the political drama surrounding the pandemic: protests, racism, and the election. The Internet and media fuel the conflict, division, and drama. All the emotional uproar is really a distraction from the overwhelming sorrow and fear we all feel. We feel helpless against the unseen power of the Coronavirus and resent the restrictions on our lives.

As the pandemic drags on, following its own timetable, we wonder when life will return to normal. In the meantime, we struggle to establish a balance in our lives. We want to feel safe, yet still live life. That is a delicate balance. We are always at risk of toppling over in one direction or another. Discouragement is a constant shadow. How can we maintain our hope in the midst of the uncertainty?

WAY OF THE CROSS

Dame Julian of Norwich provides a role model for keeping balanced. She lived in the time of the horrific death-dealing plague and suffered a critical illness herself. However, she did not ignore or diminish the suffering around her. Nor did she allow herself to be overwhelmed by it. What was her secret to keeping centered?

She tells us the answer. As Dame Julian lay dying, the priest held a crucifix in front of her face. She wrote: "Everything grew dim, until the whole room was as dark as night. The only thing I could see was the cross, which was bathed in a rather ordinary light. I couldn't figure out how it was possible that only this single object was illuminated.... By this time I was convinced that I was passing away. Suddenly, all my pain vanished, and I was whole again." (Chapter 3) Keeping her eyes focused on the cross of Jesus Christ made her whole. She then received 16 visions, which she called "showings," of God's love.

Her book, entitled *Revelations of Divine Love,* contains her reflections over 20 years on these 16 visions. It begins with her musings about Jesus' excruciating suffering on the cross. Following the medieval preoccupation with Christ's passion, Julian enumerates in almost grotesque detail the blood flowing, whipping, crowning with thorns, nailing, spear piercing, and so forth. What prevents this recounting from degenerating into morbidity are her meditations on the revelations of the abundance and graciousness of God's love. She holds in tension the opposites of sorrowful suffering and joyful love. The cross becomes an expression of God's love for us and a means for transforming our own suffering. She suggests the Black Plague is her way of the cross, destined to bring new life.

WE SUFFER WITH CHRIST

For Julian, the cross brings comfort because of our sharing in the suffering of Christ. We do not suffer alone. The Son of God accompanies us. She writes: "As I gazed upon that same crucifix, his facial expression suddenly changed to joy. The transformation of his blessed countenance transformed mine. I became as glad and as merry as I could be. And then our Beloved cheerfully suggested to my mind, 'Is there any point to your pain or your grief, now?' And I found that I was completely happy. I realized that what Christ meant to show me is that we are hanging on the cross with him right now—in our pain, in our suffering, even in our dying—and that if we willingly stay with him there, he will, by his grace, convert all our distress into delight." (Chapter 21) Further, she writes: "He wants us to realize that we never suffer alone, but always together with him, and to rest in him as our foundation." (Chapter 28)

If we feel alone with our suffering, we can easily give in to discouragement and despair. When we know that we suffer with Christ, He becomes a model for us in our anguish. Julian writes: "Christ humbly showed me his patience as he endured his cruel passion and also the joy this passion gave him because of love. He used this as a model for how we might more easily and even gladly bear our own suffering." (Chapter 73) Our natural tendency is to resent and resist what we have to suffer. We protest, "This should not be happening to me! This pandemic should not have happened!" However, the example of Christ teaches the power of love. He took up His cross out of love for us. If we accept our suffering in love, it can be transformed into joy. Then we can allow our broken hearts to open us to God and to others. Julian reminds us, "The love that made him suffer his passion is greater than all his pain." (Chapter 22)

What is the kind of love that transforms pain into joy? The cross is the gold standard of authentic love. Our society honors many counterfeit loves. For example, songs praise romance, the heart-felt passion for our soul-mate, as the height of love. But such love burns out in its own heat. Love of country, family, and even friends is celebrated as a model of dedication. But such love is selective and conditional. In contrast, the love Jesus revealed on the cross is self-sacrificing, unconditional, and universal. There are no limits to its reach, even to our enemies. It is a love that expects no return. It is a whole-hearted commitment that includes all the virtues listed in I Corinthians 13: "Love is patient, kind, not jealous…" Only such a self-denying love transforms our suffering into joy. And we experience that joy now, not just in the afterlife.

CHRIST SUFFERS WITHIN US

For Julian, the cross also brings comfort because Christ shares in our suffering. He dwells within all of us, so we all suffer together as one body. We are the suffering body of Christ in the world today, extending His compassion. She writes: "Then I saw that every impulse of loving compassion we have toward our fellow human beings is the Christ in us, and every kind of humiliation he suffered in his passion is revealed in our compassion....He wants us to know that all our pain will be transformed into blessings and honor by virtue of his passion. He wants us to realize that we never suffer alone, but always together with him, and to rest in him as our foundation." (Chapter 28)

Julian echoes the words of St. Paul: "I have been crucified with Christ. It is no longer I that live, but Christ lives within me." (Galatians 2: 20) She writes: "The knot that connects us to him is subtle and powerful and endlessly holy. And he also wants us to realize that all souls are interconnected, united by this oneness, and make holy in this holiness." (Chapter 53) Of course, the crucified Christ lives within all of us, not just a select few.

The initial pandemic refrain, "We are all in this together," is still true even though we seldom hear it these days. In fact, we have a double bond with each other. First of all, we share a bond of suffering and the desire for relief from it. All of us are grieving terrible losses. No one is spared. Some of us have been sick. Others have lost loved ones. The normal lives and financial security of all of us have been disrupted. We can see the face of the suffering Christ in everyone we meet.

The second bond we share is love and compassion. Julian writes: "I saw that in truth our Beloved is never angry, nor ever shall be, for he is God. He is good; he is life; he is truth; he is love; he is peace. His power, wisdom, and loving kindness leave no room for anger." (Chapter 46) If God dwells within us, we share His nature and life.

Who is the God who makes His residence within all of us? He is a God of love, truth, and peace, not anger. We, too, are essentially good and loving. Our suffering, then, can open our hearts in compassion to the suffering of others. All the hatred and contentiousness we experience during the pandemic violates our true nature. We forget ourselves. Gazing upon the cross of Christ, we see a display of unconditional love that reveals who we really are. Our challenge is to show up as ourselves and let our innate goodness and love shine forth.

THE CROSS AS BIRTHING

Julian presents another striking image of redemptive suffering. She addresses Jesus as our Mother, birthing us to new life. In the patriarchal society and Church of her day, just as in ours, it was a shocking revelation. She writes: "We are aware that when our mothers give birth to us we end up suffering and dying. But what is this? Our true Mother Jesus, embodiment of all love, gives us a birth that leads only to never-ending joy and eternal life. Oh, what blessing! In love, he labors to carry us inside himself, until we come to full term. Then he suffers the most painful blows and excruciating birth pangs that ever have been endured, only to die in the end. And when he had finished dying, and birthed us into endless bliss, still all this could not satisfy his wondrous love….And so now he must nourish us, which is what a mother does. The human mother can suckle the child with milk, but our beloved Mother Jesus can feed us with himself." (Chapter 60) Jesus continues to nourish us with the Eucharist, His own body and blood. Again, she writes, "In dying on the cross, he birthed us into everlasting life." (Chapter 63)

God, of course, has no gender. Yet, traditionally we refer to God the Father and God the Son, while ignoring the Divine Feminine. Julian restores the balance. She addresses the triune God as All-Power Father, All-Wisdom Son and Mother, and All-Love Spirit. What a marvelous vision of God! Jesus is like a mother nurturing us with tender love. We are created in the womb of God and given birth to new life through Jesus' labor pains. The cross symbolizes these necessary birth pangs. Like for a woman in labor, the pain is overshadowed by the joy of bringing a new life into the world.

Our suffering during the pandemic is the experience of pregnancy and labor pains. We anguish and struggle as we nurture some unknown new life within us. We feel pain but accept it. Pain is unavoidable in this birthing process. Instead, our attention is focused on the joy of bringing something new into the world. We patiently endure the losses of the present moment because of our hope for a better future.

That is the way of the cross, which is foolishness to those ignorant of God's wisdom. In our consumer society, which promotes pleasure seeking, personal success, and material accumulation for happiness, the cross is a scandal. It proclaims the need for self-denial and the acceptance of suffering as essential to a joyful life.

PAIN'S TEACHING

Only adversity gives birth to hope. The known pain opens our hearts to an unknown future if we endure it patiently. St. Paul, a man well acquainted with suffering, wrote: "We even boast of our afflictions! Affliction makes for endurance, and endurance for tested virtue, and tested virtue for hope. And this hope will not leave us disappointed." (Romans 5: 3-5) During our struggles through this pandemic, we need wise teachers like St. Paul and Julian of Norwich to guide us on the way of hope. What do they advise? They recommend the following four attitudes:

Patient endurance

Another name for suffering is lack of control. We suffer when we feel powerless over our lives. During the pandemic, we are feeling powerless over the Coronavirus and suffer terrible losses to our familiar and stable way of life. We may become sick or lose loved ones. To cope, we may try to flee the pain, ignoring it, distracting ourselves, or self-medicating. Or we may allow ourselves to be overwhelmed by it.

Jesus' Gethsemane prayer suggests another attitude: patient acceptance. As he faced death, He prayed, "Father, if it is your will, take this cup from me; yet not my will but yours be done." (Luke 22: 42) The first step of Alcoholics Anonymous echoes this attitude. Recovery begins only after admitting powerlessness over our condition and the unmanageability of our lives. Likewise, the journey of hope begins with the patient acceptance of unavoidable suffering.

Humility

Humility is truth, seeing ourselves without illusions. It is seeing and accepting ourselves as we are, not as we wish to be. During the pandemic, we protest, "This should not be happening!" We entertain high expectations about who we are and how our lives should be. The disruption caused by COVID-19 does not fit in with our planned lives. The virus exposes our vulnerability, and we hate it.

St. Paul encourages us to assume the humble attitude of Jesus Christ. He described it as "self-emptying."Christ did not grasp equality with God, but humbly became human and submitted to death on a cross. (Philippians 2: 1-11) The path to hope requires that we humbly acknowledge and accept our vulnerability. We can learn from our sadness and fear what we cling to for happiness, our attachments. What we hate losing reveals what we love, perhaps excessively. Such humility will also lead to an honest self-examination of what is really important in our lives and what lasts. We then develop tested virtue.

Compassion

As noted earlier, the word *compassion* comes from two root words: *cum* (with) and *passio* (suffering). It means, "suffering with another." During the pandemic, we may become preoccupied with our own misery and withdraw for self-protection. Our suffering may close us off from others. We indulge in self-pity. Jesus' words on the cross reveal the divine face of compassion. He prayed, "Father, forgive them; they do not know what they are doing." (Luke 23: 34). In the throes of death, Jesus did not focus on His pain, but reached out in forgiveness.

None of us suffers alone. We live in a wounded world, marked by unspeakable suffering. The media brings the pain of those around the world into our living rooms, making us aware of the reality that we are one human family. We suffer together and seek relief together. Our suffering can open our hearts to empathize and reach out to others in need like ourselves. Hope emerges as we walk together the path toward new life.

Surrender

Surrendering, opening ourselves to another, is an act of trust. During the pandemic, trust is a scarce commodity. The Internet, politicians, and media spread so much misinformation that we cannot distinguish truth and falsehood. We do not know whom to believe. Worst of all, we lack confidence in ourselves to manage all the uncertainty. Jesus' last words on the cross were words of trust, "Father, into your hands I commend my spirit." (Luke 23: 46) Jesus had unconditional confidence in His Father's love that enabled Him to surrender himself whole-heartedly in death as in His life.

To overcome mistrust, we, too, must encounter and surrender ourselves to God dwelling in our hearts. As Alcoholics Anonymous affirms, we need to surrender to a Power Greater than ourselves to maintain our sanity. As we exercise patient endurance, humility, and compassion during these trying times, we surprise ourselves at the inner strength we discover through God's grace. Hope springs eternal from the experience of that strength.

A traumatic event, such as the pandemic, attacks the body, mind, and spirit. Besides medical and mental illness, we are at risk in our suffering to despair. Our struggles may lack meaning. Mystic, Julian of Norwich, in writing about her private revelations during the Black Plague, witnessed a path of hope through adversity. She proclaimed that the path to hope intersected with Jesus' way of the cross. We do not suffer alone. Our suffering is joined with that of Christ and the whole world. By contemplating the crucifix, which reveals divine love and authentic human love, we can keep centered. By embracing our current suffering with patience, humility, and compassion, we can come to hope, like Julian, that "all will be well, and all will be well, and every kind of thing shall be well."

CHAPTER EIGHT

QUARANTINE

"This is a moment to think big, to rethink our priorities—what
we value, what we want, what we seek—and to commit to
act in our daily life on what we have dreamed of."
—Pope Francis

We Catholics believe in the value of making retreats to reflect more deeply on the meaning of our lives. We follow in the footsteps of Jesus who made a 40-day retreat in the desert before preaching the Good News.

I received an unexpected call one night from a patient I saw earlier in the day. She said, "I've been exposed to someone with COVID and took a test. I'll know the results in two days. I'm so sorry I disrupted your life." I thanked her for telling me and told her there was no need to apologize. She felt what I had observed in several of my patients who had become infected, "COVID shame." Those who contract the disease feel judged by others for being negligent and causing their own sickness. Mostly, however, they are judging themselves for something they believe they could have avoided. After the call, I decided to put myself in quarantine and work from home. Two days later, she told me she tested positive.

Her call should not have been so unexpected. Since the pandemic hit our shores, I decided to continue my therapy practice from the office. Many of my patients choose phone sessions but some prefer to meet face-to-face with the recommended precautions. Because of the contagiousness of the Coronavirus and its hiding in the asymptomatic, I knew it would just be a matter of time before I was exposed.

During the shutdown/slowdown, I took precautions and put my life on pause. I stopped meeting with family and friends and going to restaurants and other entertainment events. I postponed travel and vacations. I am fortunate, however, that I can continue working with adequate safety measures, unlike so many who are suffering devastating financial losses. While my outer life has slowed down, my inner life is on overdrive.

These 2½ years I have spent more time reading, writing, and reflecting. I am trying to make sense of what is going on in our world and in our psyches with this pandemic. I have read several books on pandemics, including *The Plague* by Albert Camus and *A Journal of the Plague Year* by Daniel Defoe. (1) Some of my patients tell me they believe God sends such plagues once every hundred years to punish us for our sins and call us to repentance.

What I have learned through my reading is that widespread infections have always been with us, and likely always will. As human beings of only 7½ billion, we are guests on a planet with trillions upon trillions of micro-organisms. Over the centuries, our reactions to the epidemics have been similar. We quarantine and protest the restrictions on our lives. The best and the worst in us come out—generosity and selfishness, bravery and cowardice, acceptance and rebellion. Human nature does not change.

For example, I was struck by the horror and beauty of Daniel Defoe's account of the black plague in London in 1665 where nearly half the population died. He told numerous stories of how individuals and families struggled in the face of imminent death by the "distemper." He called the plague "a visitation" by an unwelcome guest who would eventually leave. His brother tried to persuade him to leave the city for safety, but Daniel refused. He wrote, "It came to me one morning… that it was the will of Heaven I should not go. It immediately followed in my thoughts that if it really was from God that I should stay, He was able effectually to preserve me in the midst of all the death and danger that would surround me." (p. 6) Leaving for him would be "flying from God" and eventually bring retribution. He often prayed Psalm 91, "I will say of the Lord, He is my refuge and fortress." Defoe believed the plague was sent from God to awaken us from our complacency. It was a call to repentance.

Defoe considered it his divine mission to write about the plague. He wandered throughout the city, listening to people's stories and gathering information. He spent much time alone reading and writing his memorandums and private meditations. He often made personal retreats at home, "which time I spent in the most serious thankfulness for my perseveration and the preservation of my family, and the constant confession of my sins, giving myself up to God every day, and applying to Him with fasting, humiliation, and meditation." (p. 40)

Defoe is an inspiration to me as I continue my work and spend more time alone than is my custom.

RETREAT FOR RENEWAL

Not only the pandemic, but also life itself. sometimes require that we quarantine ourselves. For example, my patient Nancy is married to a man who has Alzheimer's. His cognitive abilities have been deteriorating for some time. Now she witnesses daily the gradual disappearance of her soulmate. Nancy stays home with him, answers his repetitive questions, and cares for his every need. He has become childlike and clings to her. They do not go out much because he becomes confused and agitated in unfamiliar circumstances.

Nancy told me she sustains herself with fantasies of being on a Florida beach, her favorite place in the world. She loves the warmth, closeness to nature, and the endless blue of the ocean. She enjoys walking the sandy beaches where she feels like a carefree child again. Together, we reflected on sandy places, the beach and the desert. Both places have an excess of sun, which both brightens and burns. Both are expansive and boundless in their natural beauty. The ocean extends to the limitless horizon, and the desert sky holds countless stars. In our imaginations, the beach is where we vacation and have fun, whereas the desert suggests the harshness and dryness of purification. Nancy confesses, "Even though this is the most difficult thing I have ever done in my life, I would not be anyplace else than here with my husband." At home, she is on a desert retreat.

The word *quarantine* is interesting in its reminiscences of the desert. We have faced plagues since the beginning of recorded history. Before modern medicine and the knowledge of germs, we developed a contagion theory based upon observations. The practice developed of separating the sick from the well. Initially, 30 days was considered sufficient. However, during the black plague in 14th century Europe, the time of separation was extended to 40 days.

The word *quarantine* comes from two Italian words, (40) and *giorni* (days). The European culture in the Middle Ages was thoroughly Christian. The number 40 imaginatively connected the people with Jesus who fasted in the desert for 40 days before beginning his public ministry. It also reminded them of Moses and the Jewish people wandering in the desert for 40 years, journeying from slavery in Egypt to the freedom of the Promised Land.

The desert, like the beach, is a borderland. The desert is a dry, empty space between oases where there is water and life. The beach is on the border between the land and the sea. Both suggest a time and place of transition. We make a retreat into the desert, like Jesus and the Jews did, to prepare ourselves for new life. The new life, which we can hardly imagine, requires that we purify ourselves, face our demons, and be strengthened to take on new challenges. In the desert both Jesus and the Jewish people gained a sense of identity and mission. At the beach we relax for a while to be refreshed for the return to work.

This time of pandemic pause from our normal routines can be both a desert and a beach. The excessive time alone and together with our families can be challenging. However, it can be an opportunity for renewal of our relationships, like a vacation together on the beach. It can also be a time for deep reflection on who we are and what we value most. Being alone and quiet exposes what is hidden within our hearts. We can work to recognize and release the attachments that interfere with our happiness. Pope Francis views this "stoppage" as a moment ripe for change and conversion. He wrote, "This is a moment to dream big, to rethink our priorities—what we value, what we want, what we seek—and to commit to act in our daily life on what we have dreamed of." (2)

This pandemic pause is a time of retreat for personal renewal. We undertake the challenge of spending time alone with ourselves. Stop and listen to the deepest longings of your heart. You may enjoy reading those inspirational books you never found time before to pick up. Try the discipline of writing. Each day, take a few moments to record your thoughts in a journal. It can be your personal diary of your soul's journey through this time of trial.

Many ask what the new normal will be like after the pandemic ends. That will depend on the dreams and commitments nurtured during this global quarantine. I take heart because the Renaissance in Italy rose up from the ashes of the black plague.

CHAPTER NINE

BALANCE IN UNSTEADY TIMES

"Self-possessed, resolute, act without any thought of results, open to success or failure. This equanimity is yoga."
—Bhagavad Gita

For us Catholics, faith is the rock on which we stand during life's storms.

"I'm sick and tired of living like this. When will this pandemic ever end so I can get my life back?" is a common complaint these days. The unwelcome visitation of COVID-19 has disrupted our lives, turning us upside down. We feel forced to make adjustments against our will to safeguard our health. We resent the imposed changes, whether or not we believe they are necessary. One local celebrity tweeted, "I'm over with living under this dictatorship." She voiced what many of us feel—like helpless victims. We may experience the government as the dictator mandating unwanted restrictions or the Coronavirus itself as controlling our lives.

As a clinical psychologist working during the pandemic, I help my patients navigate their lives in these unsteady times. Many are experiencing "pandemic fatigue." They miss the freedom and pleasures of their former way of life. They feel enslaved by the restrictions on their gatherings with family and friends and breathing through masks. Worry is their constant companion. Even with the hope provided by the vaccine, uncertainty grips them about the future and what it will look like. They mourn so many losses of loved ones, time together, and financial security. Many tell me they feel like Humpty Dumpty teetering on a wall, terrified of falling and breaking apart. They say, "I feel so exhausted adjusting to so many changes, coping with so much uncertainty. I'm just trying to keep my life together."

What makes us so fatigued? What drains our energy? In this time of pause from our routines, we might expect we would be more rested. The slowdown offers an opportunity for rest and relaxation both alone and with our families. It is a break from all the usual running around. What, then, makes us so sick and tired?

I believe we are so fatigued because we are fighting ourselves. Our thinking contradicts our experience. We are experiencing the savagery of nature in the virus and our own vulnerability. We hate what is happening. We protest, "This should not be happening. I never expected anything like this. I'm not prepared." We struggle with our current reality and wish our lives would be different. So many hopes are being dashed. So many desires are unmet. So many fears have been realized. We are so exhausted because we hate what we have and seek what we cannot have now. When we fight reality, we will lose 100% of the time, and drain ourselves in the process.

What can stop the energy drain and fatigue? How can we again energize ourselves?

EQUANIMITY

What can help us keep our balance and restore our energy in these unsteady times is the virtue of equanimity. It is the state of mind that enables us to remain undisturbed by our experiences and emotions. The word come from *aequus* (even) and *animus* (mind, soul). Having equanimity is like possessing an inner gyroscope that keeps us steady in shifting circumstances.

Equanimity is a traditional virtue taught by all the religious and wisdom traditions. In the Buddhist tradition, equanimity is one of the "Four Immeasurables," refuges in an impermanent world, along with loving-kindness, compassion, and joy. Christians label this patience and forbearance, one of the essential qualities of love, required to take up one's cross. The Hindu classic *Bhagavad Gita* defines it, "Self-possessed, resolute, act without any thought of results, open to success or failure. This equanimity is yoga." (2:48)

In a similar fashion, the Chinese book of wisdom *Tao Te Ching* (1) describes it, "The Master's power is like this./He lets all things come and go/effortlessly, without desire./He never expects results;/thus he is never disappointed./He is never disappointed;/thus his spirit never grows old." (55)

Marcus Aurelius, the Stoic philosopher-king, wrote in his *Meditations*, "The soul is a sphere in equilibrium. Not grasping at things beyond it or retreating inward." (11:12) He compares the balanced soul to a rock in the ocean, "To be like the rock that the waves keep crashing over. It stands unmoved and the raging sea falls still around it." (4:49) The word "Islam" comes from an Arabic word that denotes the peace that comes from total surrender and acceptance.

Our thinking has powerful consequences on the quality of our lives. If we protest reality and dwell on anger, without taking constructive action, we will suffer. The Buddhist classic *The Way of the Bodhisattva* (2) warns about the fruits of anger, "Those tormented by the pain of anger/will never know tranquility of mind—/Strangers they will be to every pleasure;/sleep departs them, they can never rest." (6:3) In contrast, the author, Shantideva, promises, "For patience in samsara brings such things/as beauty, health, and good renown./Its fruit is great longevity,/the vast contentment of a universal king." (6:134)

The virtue of equanimity is particularly important because we live in an age of anxiety. Our age is marked by speed and insecurity. Changes in life occur more rapidly than at any other time in history. The rate is increasing with advances in technology and communication. We can hardly keep up with each new version of the I-Phone. We are challenged to make constant adjustments to these changes. The continual demands counter our desire for the security of familiar routines. Often we feel unbalanced, unsure and inadequate to cope. And this pandemic has thrust many of us onto the outer edge of our coping ability. No wonder we are so fatigued.

The antidote to this teeter-tottering fatigue is to cultivate the virtue of equanimity. A virtue is a good habit. As a habit, it is learned and must be cultivated by daily practice, ongoing effort, and discipline. A vice is a bad habit, which must be unlearned for the virtue to emerge. How can we cultivate equanimity? The wisdom traditions offer these four recommendations:

1. Observe passing thoughts.
2. Focus on the present moment.
3. Do what is necessary.
4. Stay grounded in nature.

OBSERVE PASSING THOUGHTS

Automatic negative thoughts (ANTs) disturb our peace of mind. Thoughts of protest against what we are experiencing in the moment arise. We do not like an aspect of our reality and rebel against the experience. We complain to ourselves and to anyone who will listen, "This should not be! My life should be different than it is!" Marcus Aurelius reminds us, "That things have no hold on the soul. They stand there unmoving, outside it. Disturbance comes only from within—from our own perceptions."(4:3) If we dwell on our critical judgments and nurture our anger, we suffer. We entertain thoughts that contradict the reality of our lived experience. We engage in a war against ourselves. It is a war we cannot win. It ends with the defeat of our happiness and wellbeing. We are the primary casualty.

The first medicine and vaccine for the pandemic fatigue that results from this no-win battle is quiet reflection. The *Tao Te Ching* recommends that we spend time in silence and observe our passing thoughts. The author, Lao-tzu, teaches that the practice will help center us and keep us from a fragmented confusion. He wrote:

> "Empty your mind of all thoughts.
>
> Let your heart be at peace.
>
> Watch the turmoil of beings,
>
> but contemplate their return.
>
> Each separate being in the universe
>
> returns to the common source.
>
> Returning to the source is serenity.
>
> If you don't realize the source,
>
> you stumble in confusion and sorrow." (16)

During the pandemic, we have spent more time alone because of the restrictions on social gatherings. We Americans are a gregarious people, uncomfortable being alone with ourselves. Some of my patients complain, "When I spend too much time alone, I'm flooded with negative thoughts." However, if we take the risk and enter the silence, what will we discover?

We will observe how our thoughts arise from some unknown source and simply come and go. They have no more substance than a cloud. They evaporate unless we give them weight by believing in their truthfulness, their correspondence with reality. We will notice that we automatically put thoughts together to construct stories. These internal narratives become the maps for understanding ourselves and the world. We sense how much energy we invest in these story-maps, use them to guide our behavior, and derive both pleasure and pain from them.

However, with our wise, observing mind we realize that these maps are not the real landscape. Thoughts are not facts. They must be investigated for their truth value against our lived experience. If we blindly accept their validity without intelligent discernment, they can lead us to act in ways that harm ourselves and others.

One persistent thought is what we imagine our future should be. We think we know what is ultimately good or bad for us. A well-known Eastern story exposes the illusion of our preoccupation with outcomes. A poor farmer's horse ran off one day. All his neighbors offered their condolences, but his father said, "We'll see." After a few months the horse returned with another horse of excellent stock. All his neighbors offered their congratulations, but his father said, "We'll see." The two horses bred, and the family became rich with their fine horses. The farmer's son spent much of his time riding them. Then, one day he fell off and broke his hipbone. All his neighbors offered their condolences, but his father said, "We'll see." Another year passed, and a war broke out. All the able-bodied young men were drafted, and 90% of them died in the war. Who can know what is good fortune or a disaster? Who can tell how events will change?

Quiet time alone can energize us by reconnecting us with our lived experience and wise minds.

FOCUS ON THE PRESENT MOMENT

The mind is timeless. It wanders freely, back and forth, in the past, present, and future. However, in this time of pandemic stress, we can become fixated on the past or future to escape the present. We may engage in "if only" thinking about the past, regretting decisions made and suffering consequences unforeseen and unwanted. We may be filled with sorrow over the many losses we have experienced because of the pandemic—so many precious times together lost. Then, our minds may jump to the unknown future which frightens us. We engage in "what if" thinking about the future, imagining the worst. Worry about life after COVID-19 may torment us. We ask, "Will we ever recover all that we have lost?" Dwelling on the past and future, which do not exist, drains our energy to be fully involved in the present moment. Only the present moment is real.

A second medicine to relieve pandemic fatigue is focusing our attention on the present moment. That reorients us to reality so we are not lost in flights of fantasy about the past or future. A Zen saying reminds us of this truth: "Nothing happens next. This is it!" The future will take care of itself if we pay full attention to the demands of the present. The *Bhagavad Gita* invites us to live fully in the present with equanimity by letting go of our expectations, fears, and desires: "With no desire for success, no anxiety about failure, indifferent to results, he burns up his actions in the fire of wisdom....There is nothing he expects, nothing he fears. Serene, free from possessions, untainted, acting with the body alone." (4:19, 21)

We ground ourselves by standing firmly in the reality of the present. Putting energy into worry about future outcomes, success, or failure distracts us from addressing the demands of the present. If we are fully present to ourselves and our situation in life, we will stay balanced. Only fear of and hope for the future can unsteady us. Living out of desire, fear, or hope takes us out of reality into flights of fantasy. We even imagine ourselves as separate from the universe. The *Tao* echoes the message of the *Gita*:

"Success is as dangerous as failure.

Hope is as hollow as fear.

What does it mean that success is as dangerous as failure?

Whether you go up the ladder or down it,

your position is shaky.

When you stand with your two feet on the ground,

you will always keep your balance.

What does it mean that hope is as hollow as fear?

Hope and fear are both phantoms

that arise from thinking of the self.

When we don't see the self as self,

what do we have to fear?

See the world as your self.

Have faith in the way things are.

Love the world as your self;

then you can care for all things." (13)

During stressful times, we will inevitably have periods of sorrow, anxiety, hope, and joy, at times intense. However, when we live beyond desire, hope, and fear, we can regain our balance. Living fully in the present, we embrace all of our experience, excluding nothing, even the painful times. We refuse to run away from any aspect of our experience. Equanimity gives us confidence so we can avoid denying or getting carried away by any reaction. Peace will come when we willingly accept moments of both joy and sorrow, feel our reactions, learn from them, and let them go. We need not be puppets, pulled by the strings of our emotions.

We stand on firm ground, connected to the universe, when we focus on the present.

DO WHAT IS NECESSARY

In these stressful times, we are restless and exhausted because we try to do too much and too little. Our activity level is unbalanced. One woman complained, "I have so much to do working from home, home-schooling the children, and taking care of the house. I feel overwhelmed all the time. I'll never catch up." She is overwhelmed, not because of her circumstances, but because of what she expects of herself. She is trying too hard. Some others feel overextended because they feel so empty and restless without their usual activities. Instead, they chase after another life in their head. Still others live in the grip of sadness or fear and withdraw within ourselves. Another woman told me, "I feel so depressed all I want to do is sleep."

A third antidote depends on a realistic assessment of what needs to be done in the moment. Instead of chasing after a life we do not have, Marcus Aurelius recommends that we focus our efforts at doing what is necessary in our current life. He wrote: "If you seek tranquility, do less. Or (more accurately) do what's essential—what the *logos* (mind) of a social being requires, and in the requisite way. Which brings a double satisfaction: to do less, better. Because most of what we say and do is not essential. If you can eliminate it, you'll have more time, and more tranquility. Ask yourself at every moment, 'Is this necessary?' But we need to eliminate unnecessary assumptions as well. To eliminate the unnecessary actions that follow." (4:24) His advice is to simplify our lives, focusing on the essential, on what is really important.

The pandemic has been a time of renunciation, of eliminating many activities, for most of us. We have been deprived of many of our treasured activities, especially in socializing and entertaining. We assumed we needed to keep busy to be happy. Many of us feel miserable because of the loss of these routines. This pause invites us to question assumptions about what makes us happy. We can ask ourselves, "Do I really need to be doing all this to be happy? Is what I'm doing really necessary?"

A middle-aged patient of mine, who has been plagued with anxiety her whole life, told me how unexpectedly calm she has been during the pandemic. She said, "I'm focusing on this small square plot of land that is my life. I'm cooking meals, cleaning the house, doing laundry, and enjoying my family." She related that she discovered she does not need to be running around shopping and going to restaurants and movies to be happy. She has simplified her life and is content. She has everything she needs in the confines of her home.

Our culture teaches that having and doing more is better. However, that is only the biased message of a materialist, consumer society. The pandemic gives us an opportunity to examine the societal message we assume to be true. If we look closely at the relentless chase after new experiences, we realize how much it disturbs our peace of mind. Especially now, we exhaust ourselves desiring things we cannot have. The *Tao Te Ching* presents an alternative view, reflected in the wisdom of Marcus Aurelius. Doing less can be more. Lao-tzu wrote:

> Less and less do you need to force things,
>
> until finally you arrive at non-action.
>
> When nothing is done,
>
> nothing is left undone.
>
> True mastery can be gained
>
> by letting things go their own way.
>
> It can't be gained by interfering. (48)

Lao-tzu is not suggesting idleness but a dynamic awareness of the demands of the moment. If we are fully engaged in our life and work we will know what needs to be done. Undistracted by our cravings for more, we will focus on what is most important.

The wisdom of the *Tao* and of the Stoics is repeated in the Serenity Prayer: "God, grant me the serenity to accept the things I cannot change, courage to change the things I can, and the wisdom to know the difference." Keeping balanced requires an accurate assessment of different realms of responsibility, what belongs to God, to others, and to ourselves. If we overreach with unrealistic expectations, we set ourselves up for failure and frustration. We cannot change the course of nature, such as the pandemic. That belongs to God. Neither are we responsible for others' behavior. They are. Serenity will come from accepting these limits. However, we can alter our own thinking, attitudes, and behaviors to benefit all. That is our personal realm of responsibility, which requires courage and wisdom to fulfill. We ask ourselves, "Whose business is this?" We need clear insight and wisdom to recognize where our responsibility begins and ends. Marcus Aurelius affirms, "To love only what happens, what was destined. No greater harmony." (7:57) This is an invitation to be our natural selves and responsibly pursue our deepest values.

We live a balanced life when we simply do what is necessary.

STAY GROUNDED IN NATURE

"I can't sleep at night," John complained. "The next day I feel miserable, tired, and irritable." I asked, "What keeps you awake?" He responded, "I can't shut off my brain. I keep thinking about what I have to do, and I worry. I don't know how to relax." John is not alone with this complaint. We imagine there is so much to do and not enough time to do it. Especially during the pandemic, we cannot shut off our worrying brain. We are living more in our minds these days than in our bodies. The result is that we cannot relax, and we wear ourselves out.

Many of my younger patients complain about boredom. They feel like caged animals at home. They miss hanging out with their friends. Some say, "I don't want to miss out on anything." They admit being driven by

"FOMO," the fear of missing out. There is so much they want and not enough time to get it. Keeping active and chasing the excitement of new experiences act like a drug to make them feel alive.

The fourth remedy to regain our peace of mind is to connect with our bodies. Siddhartha Gautama, who became the Buddha (Enlightened One), revealed its importance. After the shock of encountering those who were old, sick, and dead, the young prince Siddhartha decided to devote his life to the relief of suffering. He then undertook a 6-year personal search to discover the secret to freedom from suffering. He studied the ancient Scriptures, meditated, and fasted until near death. Eventually, he decided to enter a forest and simply sit under a tree and be quiet. He stopped and did nothing. He went to nature to discover its truths. While he sat, Mara (The Deceitful One) tempted him with sensual delights and threats and mocked his mission. Siddhartha responded by touching the earth, calling upon it as his witness. Then, he became enlightened, the Buddha.

He reminded us that we are born of the earth, made from its dust. One day we shall return to the earth, which is both our womb and tomb. The word *human* comes from the Latin word *humus* (earth). *Humus* is also the root word for humility. When we are lost in our thoughts about how we believe life should be, we entertain grandiose ideas. Pride takes over. We resist our earthly existence, thinking we know what is best. Our lack of humility, our lack of acceptance of our fragile, impermanent nature, does not improve our lot. Instead, it estranges us from our natural selves.

The earth is our home, and we dwell in our bodies. Mother Nature gave us birth and continually nourishes us. We exist because we are in a constant interchange with the universe. The *Tao Te Ching* reminds us of this often-forgotten truth: "The Tao (The Way, Truth, and Life) is called the Great Mother:/empty yet inexhaustible,/it gives birth to infinite worlds./It is always present within you./You can use it any way you want." (6) The limitless energy of life flows through us and the

BEING CATHOLIC IN TROUBLED TIMES | 83

whole universe, connecting us with all living creatures. Life is such a precious gift. We enjoy the miracle of life and share in its abundance. Mother Nature is present within us, continually creating and sustaining our wellbeing.

Since social gatherings have been restricted, I have reacquainted myself with Mother Nature. I found several parks in my area and take walks each day. I am able to set aside my "wild monkey mind" and relax with the scenery. I open my eyes, ears, nose, mouth, and skin to the beauty around me. I indulge my senses and experience my body as alive. Gratitude for the miraculous abundance and beauty of life often fills my heart. What more do I need? The experience of the Buddha and the words of the *Tao* resonate within me: "Be content with what you have;/rejoice in the way things are./When you realize there is nothing lacking,/the whole world belongs to you." (44)

Staying grounded in nature makes us feel alive and refreshed.

During stressful times, our lives are out of balance, upside-down. Our normal routines are upended. We feel lost and confused. What unsettles us most, however, is not the invasion of COVID-19 but our attitude towards this event. We hate what is happening, resist its reality, and engage in a war within ourselves. Nevertheless, this stressful period offers us the opportunity to uncover a deeper harmony. We can cultivate the virtue of equanimity and learn to find the power within ourselves to restore tranquility. That serenity of mind will radiate outwards to create a renewed harmony in our troubled world that cries out for peace.

CHAPTER TEN

DIFFICULT CONVERSATIONS

"Hate never overcomes hate. Only love overcomes hate.
That is the eternal law."
—The Buddha

We Catholics believe in the Church and the Eucharist as the Body of Christ. We feed each other to stay alive and well.

Conversations these days can be extremely difficult. Within society, we suffer the residue of a contentious election. Many still believe the election was stolen and refuse to accept the results. The pandemic lingers on. Different groups disagree on the best approach for the recovery of our physical and economic health as a nation. Democrats and Republicans have different agendas and engage in acrimonious debates with each other. Both sides of the aisle refuse to compromise. Black Americans protest systemic racism and demand to be heard, while a significant number of Whites push back out of fear of losing power and status. Regarding the pandemic, many Americans mistrust the vaccine, refuse to wear masks, and question the need for social distancing, especially at the cost of economic prosperity. The disagreeableness spills over into many of our relationships. Family members refuse to discuss politics to maintain civility. Friendships end over differing political ideas. Neighbors avoid each other.

What complicates these conversations is our intransigence. Many of us hold rigid ideas and will not be budged from our opinions. We know we are right and refuse to listen to alternative views. Others are simply wrong. Our minds are closed. What further complicates our pseudo-dialogues is that some of our rigidly held notions have little grounding in reality. There is no evidence, just a gut level certainty of their truth. Yet, many of us cling to these baseless beliefs with a stubbornness that suggests a paranoid mindset.

As mentioned previously, the word *paranoid* comes from two root words: *para* (beside) and *nous* (mind, thought). The paranoid mind creates an alternative universe separate from consensually-held reality based on evidence. This mindset can degenerate from biased, to distorted, to delusional thinking that can reach clinical levels of severity as it becomes more rigid and out of touch with reality. It is driven by a fantasy, a wish, that reality would be different than it is.

The paranoid mind is trapped in a negative thought loop. It lacks the capacity to stand back and question its assumptions about reality. Instead, it generates elaborate conspiracy theories to justify its ideas. For example, some conspiracy theories circulating today are that China created COVID-19, the pandemic is a hoax, the vaccine causes genetic mutations, the election is a fraud, climate change is a hoax, and so forth. Those who are paranoid mistrust any authority that challenges their firmly believed ideas—Democrats, Trump-supporters, scientists, the media, and so forth.

With the current prevalence of mistrust and paranoid thinking, how can we engage in fruitful dialogue? How can we talk with someone who has a closed mind?

PARANOID PETER

A patient, whom I shall call Peter, answered these questions for me. He taught me how to communicate with someone with fixed, delusional beliefs. We began meeting regularly for therapy several years ago. He came to see me because his anxiety kept him awake at night. As he talked, it became clear how much fear ruled his life. He felt tense, ready to fight, because he believed others were trying to take advantage of him. He trusted no one. He lived on high alert and watched his surroundings carefully. Peter admitted he was paranoid and that he had a sixth sense to recognize that quality in others. "It takes one to know one," he said.

During therapy, we discussed how he became so guarded. Peter saw his father as an anxious man with a quick temper. He showed little affection and disciplined harshly, as did his father. His mother was sickly, depressed, and often absent. Peter did not believe he could count on either parent and became a loner. He rebelled in high school and used drugs. Later, he sold drugs and spent some time in prison for his illegal entrepreneurship. In prison, his mistrust grew. However, beneath his tough façade, Peter craved the love he never received growing up. He longed to connect with people.

During treatment, Peter was learning to get in touch with his vulnerability and desire for intimacy. His hyper-vigilance never left him, but he learned not to let his fear control his life. Peter became close friends with a younger man, Joe, whom he saw as the son he never had. He noticed that paranoia was a bond they shared. Joe loved guns and saw them as necessary for his safety. He supported President Trump because he saw him as the protector of his Second Amendment right to bear arms. Joe also believed the recent election was stolen.

Peter was obsessed with politics and was well versed in conspiracy theories. He considered himself a liberal and loved to debate. He enjoyed provoking people with his ideas. I asked him how he communicated with Joe since their points of view were so different.

Peter explained, "I respect Joe's point of view even though I disagree with him and see his crazy thinking. I don't argue with him or try to persuade him to think differently. After all, we are all biased. I don't have all the answers. I realize that, like for me, fear and anger, not logic, drive his thinking. He believes he must protect his family with guns. Without a gun, he would feel unsafe. Sometimes, he becomes angry when he talks about politics, especially gun control. I just stay calm and listen. For me, our relationship is more important than our different ideas about politics. We are friends, and I want us to trust one another. I think I am influencing his negative thinking by being positive. I see his fear like a hardened clod of mud. I keep pouring the water of positivity over it so it slowly dissolves."

OPENING A DIALOGUE

Peter's response showed me a way to keep an open dialogue with someone trapped in the prison of fixed or delusional thinking. Paranoia is seductive. It takes awareness and effort to avoid being caught up in the drama and assuming the role of enemy. The following suggestions are seven steps for keeping a dialogue open:

1. Respect the Person.

Any true dialogue must begin with mutual personal respect. Peter reminds us to separate the person from the opinion. The bond of the relationship is more important than the differing ideas. Unfortunately, those with a paranoid mindset reverse these priorities. Communication is difficult unless we agree with them. They value their false beliefs more than the relationship.

Martin Buber, the Jewish philosopher, observed two different ways of relating: person-to-person (I-Thou) and person-to-object (I-It). An idea, such as a paranoid thought, is just an object in the mind. It is not truth, merely a reflection about it. Those who are paranoid become obsessively attached to the objects in their mind. They firmly believe what they think is "the Truth." Their primary loyalty is to their delusion. Without knowing it, perhaps in all sincerity, they live in a mental prison of the reality they create there. In communicating, others are an audience expected to listen and agree. If anyone disagrees, they become the enemy in their internal drama. They seek others who will mirror their distorted ideas to validate them. In short, their relationships are of an I-It, person-to-object, quality.

If we want to open an authentic dialogue eventually, our goal must be to strive for an I-Thou, person-to-person, relationship. Persons are free, conscious subjects who shape their own lives. Authentic dialogue involves the free exchange of ideas between persons who have their own opinions. The conversation is between persons who freely think what they want and explore truth together. The participants relish the unique ideas of others so they can enlarge their view of reality. To respect persons involves acknowledging their freedom to be themselves, think their own thoughts, indulge their own tastes, follow their own inclinations, and make decisions on their own. It honors their separateness and independence. In fact, they are free to believe whatever they want even if it is false.

Persons and ideas are separate. We may love the person but hate his or her ideas. When Jesus was on the cross, he prayed, "Father, forgive them for they know not what they do."(Luke 23: 34) Jesus was the Way, the Truth, and the Life. They killed him, imagining they could murder Truth. Jesus did not condemn them because he loved them even though they persecuted him. He forgave them for their ignorance. In the same way, we do not condemn those who cling to delusions, murdering the truth. We do not judge them as acting out of malice. Most likely, they are ignorant, ignoring the truth hidden in plain sight. They are slaves to falsehoods, suffering under the weight of it, and need our compassion.

2. Don't Argue.

Peter astutely observed that paranoid thinking is driven by fear and anger, not logic. Those with a paranoid mindset really feel powerless. They feel wronged by life in some way and are fearful and angry. They compensate by developing delusions that give them a sense of security and even superiority. They gather with like-minded thinkers to feel validated, safe, and strong. They stubbornly cling to their beliefs, which make them feel powerful. Any disagreement is perceived as a personal attack, which must be defended at all costs. Any debate degenerates into a hostile test of wills.

We imagine we see clearly the error of their thinking and the terrible consequences. With the best of intentions, we want to rescue them. We want them to return to consensually-shared reality. Because we see ourselves as rational people, we may engage them in debate, using facts and logic. Soon, we experience futility, frustration, and confusion. We feel powerless and lost in their hall of mirrors.

I have been caught up in the misery-go-round of debate more times than I like to admit and painfully learned its futility. For example, I attempted a rational discussion with a friend who firmly believed the election was stolen. It became a righteous cause for him to protest. I asked, "How do you know? What's the evidence?"

He responded, "There are thousands of affidavits by people who observed illegal behavior, and the voting machines were fixed."

Being rational, I said, "Of course, fraud cannot be tolerated and must be investigated. We have a Justice system to investigate and a Court system to adjudicate the evidence. Didn't the U.S. Attorney General and dozens of courts review the evidence and decide there was no fraud?"

He calmly responded, "The evidence was hidden, and the Justice Department and Courts did not do their jobs. They are part of the conspiracy."

Stalemate! I knew that nothing could disprove his firmly lodged belief. I was not about to change my mind, lie to myself, and say the election was a fraud.

The most reasonable tack, understanding the paranoid mindset, is to avoid debate. We should not keep quiet, either, because that would imply consent to the untruth. We can simply say, "I don't see the situation in the same way. This is how I understand it." And then let it go. The Chinese wisdom text, the *Tao Te Ching*, offers a war strategy that can be used in attempted dialogues with people of fixed ideas. It is a "wait and see" tactic:

> The generals have a saying:
> "Rather than make the first move
> it is better to wait and see.
> Rather than advance an inch
> it is better to retreat a yard."
> This is called
> going forward without advancing,
> pushing back without using weapons. (69)

3. Stay Calm.

We wait and see until we understand what lies underneath the paranoid thinking. Meanwhile, the challenge is to stay calm. As Peter pointed out, the paranoia is driven by fear and anger. The anger soon becomes evident in any discussion. Whatever the topic, a negative atmosphere soon fills the room. Those with a paranoid mindset believe they have been wronged in life. They complain and blame others for their misery. They feel like victims in a world populated by persecutors. Their simmering anger erupts when we disagree on topics sensitive to them.

A casual conversation may then seem like a mine field. We may suddenly trigger an angry reaction by a harmless comment. Those of a paranoid mindset project their anger onto the world and constantly fear being attacked. As a way of trying to stay ahead of the expected aggression, they become aggressive. They make pre-emptive strikes to protect themselves from their imagined adversaries.

It is difficult not to engage when we feel blamed, attacked, or demeaned for holding different views. If we are drawn into the battle, we risk becoming angry and mirroring our threatened dialogue partner. An endless spiral of escalating anger ensues.

Dr. Martin Luther King, Jr., the civil rights leader, wrote to bolster himself and his followers, "'You must not harbor anger,' I admonished myself. 'You must be willing to suffer the anger of the opponent and yet not return anger. You must not become bitter. No matter how emotional your opponents are, you must be calm.'" (1)

There is a traditional Buddhist story that suggests a detached attitude, not taking the anger personally, to remain calm. One day, the Buddha was walking across a plot of land when a man came up and angrily started shaking his fist in the Buddha's face, saying he had no right to be walking there. The Buddha looked at the man and said, "Tell me, if you prepared a lovely gift for someone, and you reached out to give it to them but they refused to accept it, to whom would the gift belong?" "To me, of course," the man replied. "Just so," the Buddha said. "I'm not accepting the gift of your anger. Therefore, it remains with you."

4. Self-Examine.

We become so outraged and hooked by those with delusional thinking because they show us our shadow. We look into the mirror, and the enemy we see is us. Our pride makes us believe we are rational, reasonable, and noble. We can become judgmental, imagining we are superior to those in the prison of paranoia.

However, as Freud observed, we, too, possess a drop of intellect in a sea of emotion. Unconscious drives also shape our thinking, reacting, and behaving. Fear, sadness, and anger often possess us. Our thinking is biased, often distorted, and sometimes bordering on delusional. Our unmet needs and fantasies, which we can glimpse in our dreams, motivate much of our behavior. We are not as different from our paranoid dialogue partners as we imagine. The antidote to our hubris is to give up taking others' moral inventories and focus on our own. That requires honesty, courage, and humility.

Dr. Martin Luther King was a master at confronting the delusional thinking of racism. In the face of hatred and violence, he insisted on maintaining a calm attitude and a nonviolent response. He was a realist and acknowledged that the civil war between blacks and whites raged within the hearts of us all. He wrote in his autobiography, "Life is a continual story of shattered dreams....And in every one of us, there's a war going on. It's a civil war. I don't care who you are, I don't care where you live, there is a civil war going on in your life. And every time you set out to be good, there's something pulling on you, telling you to be evil. It's going on in your life. Every time you set out to love, something keeps pulling on you, trying to get you to hate. Every time you set out to be kind and say nice things about people, something is pulling on you to be jealous and envious and to spread gossip about them. There's a civil war going on." (pp. 356-58) The same conflicts that inhabit the angry, violent delusional people tear us apart inside.

5. Self-Care.

Attempting to dialogue with someone with a closed mind can drain us of our life energy. We feel exhausted and can easily give up in despair. Further, the atmosphere of negativity and contentiousness seeps into our psyches. The anxiety and anger of those around us are contagious. Experts comment on the increase in clinical depression and anxiety, substance abuse, and deaths of despair among all age groups in these trying times.

Bandy X. Lee, a forensic psychiatrist, recently wrote a book analyzing President Trump and our national situation (2). She observed three groups in our society today with differing relationships to truth. She said a third of the population are locked into delusional thinking and live in a hall of mirrors with those who reflect back their own prejudiced thinking. They follow their leader and listen to selective news sources that reinforce their conspiracy notions. Another third resign themselves to not knowing and disengage from the political arena. They are swamped by the tidal wave of information from the social media. They say, "Everyone has his own opinion. Truth is relative, anyway." The final third are composed of those who continue to hold on to the idea of knowable truth. They insist on the difference between true and false, good and evil. They believe we can arrive at a reasonable (though not absolute) certainty about what is true by conscientious investigation and thoughtful reflection.

Those of us who choose to believe in the knowability of truth and stand up against falsehood can feel overwhelmed at times, which is only natural. There is an adage in medical circles, "In an emergency, take your own pulse first." In these days, the need for self-care takes on a greater urgency than ever if we are to maintain our balance. The 12 Step programs of recovery promote self-care with the acronym HALT: Don't be hungry, angry, lonely, or tired. To avoid relapse into illness, we must take care of our basic needs of having a proper diet, enough rest, social interaction, and emotional support.

We also need to keep ourselves spiritually centered with quiet time alone to reconnect with the Sacred, our values, and our commitments. We may spend a few minutes each day in prayer or meditation or more extended time away periodically. Mahatma Gandhi spent one day each week in silence to maintain his resolve, resilience, and resourcefulness for his nonviolent freedom campaign. We also nourish our spirit with time in nature, with the arts, with hobbies, and in wholesome entertainment. In short, we need inner peace to be peacemakers in our relationships.

6. Have Empathy.

We can begin to rebuild trust with those who have paranoid thinking by having empathy for them. Their paranoia is driven by a sense of woundedness. They have been wronged by life and feel like helpless victims. Their anger disguises their deep hurt, fear, and sadness. The hostile thinking and behavior protect them from being hurt again. Their mistrust serves a survival purpose.

Instead of arguing about what is true, we need to listen with our third ear to what is not being said. Dr. King observed after the Watts riot in 1965, "Riots are the language of the unheard." Paranoia and the resultant anger are also their cry of desperation. What do we need to hear? What suffering are they unable to put into words? How do they believe they have been wronged in life?

Dr. King reminded us of an obvious truth, "Life is a continual story of shattered dreams." The Buddha taught that the first noble truth is that life is suffering. The word he used for suffering was *dukkha*, which is the grinding of an axle in a wheel that is out of balance. The sources of our suffering are countless. Those with a paranoid mindset may have suffered unspeakable traumas in their personal lives.

Our society also has been traumatized by the pandemic, and the growing inequality between social classes has become more evident in the unequal distribution of suffering due to COVID-19. Social commentators refer to the increasing gap between the rich and the poor in the last few decades, which spawns social unrest, discontent, and violence. Some white Americans fear losing power and status with the increasing number of minorities in our country. Many workers have lost their jobs due to automation and globalization. The uneducated and unskilled suffer most the loss of social and economic mobility. Many believe the wealthy, educated elite are in control and care little about the needs of the common person. The list goes on. Until these grievances are heard and addressed, there will be no healing or fruitful dialogue.

7. Show Love.

All the spiritual traditions affirm that only love can overcome hatred. The Buddha taught, "Hate never overcomes hate. Only love overcomes hate. That is the eternal law." The Christian Scriptures affirm, "Perfect love casts out fear." (I John 4:18) The anger and fear that drive the paranoid thinking must be dissolved for openness to reality to emerge. Peter used a suggestive image to describe the process of healing. The anger and fear are like a hardened mud clod that can be slowly dissolved by gently pouring water on it. He recommended slowly drowning the negativity of paranoia with the water of positivity.

For genuine dialogue to overcome mistrust, we must be willing to be relentless in giving gestures of love. Small acts of love by listening, feeling empathy, and offering reassurance can make a difference. Dr. King urged, "Again and again, we must rise to the majestic heights of meeting physical force with soul force." (p. 225) That soul force is the power of love.

For the paranoia to dissolve, we cannot dismiss grievances as petty or entitled whining but need to take them seriously. Then, our society can begin working together to address the social and economic inequalities that divide our nation and feed the violence.

Open and honest communication, the free exchange of ideas, is the lifeblood of a nation and all relationships. Today we are dying from the lack of this nourishment. We are spilling blood in contentious, futile debates. Mistrust and loyalty to distorted views of the truth drain our vital energy. However, we can renew the life-giving flow of communication by opening our minds, hearts, and ears. The noise of hostile words and actions may deafen us to hearing the suppressed cries of desperation, the quiet murmurs of unspeakable suffering. Listening with compassion will rebuild trust and the mutual love for truth so that we can live more peacefully and abundantly together.

CHAPTER ELEVEN

THIS PANDEMIC IS THE PASSION

*"I have been crucified with Christ, and the life
I live now is not my own; Christ is living in me."*
—Galatians 2: 20

Jesus Christ is the cornerstone of our Church and our faith. We are "another Christ" in the world today.

The pandemic came like a thief in the night. It robbed us of our health, livelihood, and familiar lives. It took away our sense of security. Now, we are mourning the losses and trying to rebuild our lives.

I have continued meeting with my patients to help them cope and make sense of the disruption in their lives. To do my work, as mentioned previously, I first had to search out the meaning of these events for myself. I conscientiously watched the news and read commentaries on current events. I read about the history of pandemics and its impact on society. Camus' *The Plague* helped me understand the psychological toll of the disease. Like Daniel Defoe, who wrote *A Journal of the Plague Year* during the Black Plague in 1665 London, I began to write my own reflections on the experiences of myself and my patients. My goal was to discover its hidden meaning and ways to make it an opportunity for new life.

To cope with the COVID affliction, we have envisioned the pandemic as a war requiring bravery, service, and sacrifice. As a global pandemic, all the nations of the world united to fight a common enemy, the Coronavirus. We became allies in this life-and-death struggle. "We are all in this together" was our motto. However, as this war unfolded, the battlefields shifted. Political parties fought against each other about the best strategies. Nations vied for medical resources and vaccines. The inequities between the rich and the poor, the whites, and the people of color became more evident as the disease ravaged society. Further, there has been an ongoing personal battle within each of us as we struggle to adjust to the disruption to our lives and sense of security.

At the beginning of the pandemic, I asked my patients if they saw the shutdown as more of a prison or a retreat. Surprisingly, most were optimistic, envisioning the time with their families and away from the rat race as a retreat. However, over time, pandemic fatigue set in. It then felt more like a prison. Now, as the cases are dropping and the restrictions being lifted, we need another image to make sense of our experience. As we recover, the lingering effects to our emotional and social wellbeing cry out for healing. What image can guide our recovery? How can we discover meaning in our suffering? Where can we find relief in troubled times?

TWO DIVINE ECCENTRICS

Caryll Houselander, a British artist and mystic, provided an answer. She lived in London during the German bombings of the city. She wrote about her experience and described the suffering the residents endured. Their lives were disrupted by the air raids and war effort. Many were left homeless and destitute. Countless people were wounded and killed by the bombings. The youth were sent off into battle to face the enemy. Many did not return. In London, the city was on shutdown and blackout. People scrambled into shelters for safety during the raids. Social gatherings were forbidden. Food was rationed. The economy was in shambles. Fear seized the entire population. Nevertheless, although the people were down, they were not defeated. They rose up to care for the wounded, put out fires, and comfort each other. Front line health care workers risked their own lives to save others. Working tirelessly together, the residents rebuilt the devastated city. The picture of wartime London Houselander described resonates with our experience of the pandemic at its worst.

At the height of the attacks on London, Houselander, a devout Catholic, received three visions in which she saw the face of Christ in all people, even those considered her enemies. This revelation shaped her thinking about the war. She wrote a book about her reflections in 1941 entitled *This War is the Passion*. (1) She explained that we must look beyond the cruelty of the war and see our sharing in the suffering of Christ. She wrote, "For us, the war is the passion of Christ....Because he has made us 'other Christs,' because his life continues in each one of us, there is nothing that any one of us can suffer which is not the passion he suffered." (p. 1)

For us, the pandemic is the passion of Christ. It is our way of the cross.

Houselander repeated the insight of another great mystic considered eccentric like herself, Julian of Norwich. Julian (her real name is unknown) committed to live a life of prayerful seclusion in a church in Norwich, England. She lived in the 14th century when the Black Death was ravaging Europe. Nearly half the residents of her town died from the disease. When she was sick and near death, Julian received a revelation of God's love as she gazed upon a crucifix. A series of 16 visions, which she called showings, convinced her, that despite the devastation of the plague, "All would be well, and every kind of thing shall be well."

Her confidence was based on our sharing in the passion of Christ. She wrote, "He (Jesus) wants us to know that all our pain will be transformed into blessings and honor by virtue of his passion. He wants us to realize that we never suffer alone, but always together with him, and to rest in him as our foundation." (p. 70)

We do not suffer alone. Christ suffers with us during difficult times. We all suffer together as "other Christs."

THE DEFENSES OF THE MIND

Houselander observed that the world was suffering from a spiritual disease which spread like an epidemic. It was the disease of hatred. She saw the causes of this hatred in fear and indignant grief. We fear losing what we hold dear and grieve the losses already suffered. We indignantly protest the taking of innocent life. Fear and sorrow deteriorate into hatred and anger. She recommended prayer and a wise understanding of suffering as defenses against this sickness of the spirit.

We may protest the unfairness of what we are suffering and the loss of control over our lives. A prayerful awareness and a wise acceptance of suffering can heal us.

PRAYER

To overcome our fear, sadness, and anger, Houselander first recommended prayer. She wrote, "Prayer is a healing thing, and our first defense must begin to heal even while it fortifies us, and it must be the reserve on which we can draw over and over again." (p. 76) She described prayer as a silent, reflective attitude, and not just a multiplication of words and thoughts while kneeling. Jesus taught his disciples to pray to God in the privacy of their rooms and "not rattle on like the pagans." (Matthew 6: 6-7) Prayer is an attitude of openness to God's presence in our lives. It is resting in simple, clear, ever-present awareness and paying full attention to the richness or our experience.

One of the great benefits of prayer is that it gives us the power to think. Houselander explained, "The ability to think is essential to the second defense, which is a well-defined attitude to suffering which we are bound to think out for ourselves, if it is really to be of any use to us..." She added, "We cannot think out for ourselves unless we are capable of accepting certain knowledge, of making certain observations, of learning certain things at first hand, through experience." (p. 109). She observed that without the power of thinking, we fall prey to our circumstances, fears, and prejudices. Freedom demands that we use our discriminating intelligence to discover what is true and good for us.

During challenging times, we are not free unless we spend time in quiet reflection and use our intelligence to make wise decisions for the wellbeing of ourselves and society.

SCHOOL OF SUFFERING

According to Houselander, we have a double duty: to suffer well and to help others to suffer well. She observed that, while all suffer, people react differently to their tribulations. She commented, "Suffering does not have the same effect on everyone. Some people grow big through it; it enlarges them and sweetens them, it fills them with compassion. Others are narrowed and made bitter, personal grievances obsess them, they recall injuries that are years old, self-pity isolates them." (p. 116)

We may try to ignore the inevitable suffering of life by numbing ourselves with alcohol, drugs, or constant activity. Or we may allow ourselves to be carried away by it and fall into despair. Houselander suggested that we view our suffering through the lens of Christ in his passion. Our everyday life is the school of suffering to teach us valuable lessons.

During this pandemic, we have suffered terribly. What can we learn from it in the light of the passion?

Communion: Our suffering can isolate us, making us feel alone and abandoned by God and everyone else. Houselander reminded us that in the light of the passion Christ is suffering with all of us. She pointed out, "We begin to suffer with him….It is more than that, it is actually Christ suffering in us. We are united to him, we are one, and when his passion becomes real to us, through experience and love, then we grow aware of his presence in us." (p. 50) Through suffering, we can become closer to Christ because we know that he is present in our pain. We can also feel a bond with everyone else. No one escapes the trials of life. Christ dwells within us all in our difficult times.

Acceptance: Our natural instinct is to seek pleasure and avoid pain. We protest the darkness of our distress. We fight against it. However, Christ did not flee the cross but fully embraced it. Houselander wrote, "He (Jesus) welcomed his cross and took it up himself and put it on his shoulder to carry it. We can face the war in his spirit, not glad of suffering for suffering's sake, but glad that, since suffer we must, we can carry our share of the cross as a loving work for each other to help our common redemption." (p. 5) Rejecting the inevitable losses of our lives only increases our suffering and does not regain what was lost. Acceptance is the final liberating stage of our grief.

Humility: We indignantly protest our trials, complaining, "I should not have to put up with this!" Suffering brings us to our knees. It reminds us we are not complete masters of our lives. Houselander related that our suffering teaches us humility. She wrote, "It can help us to remember that we are part of a whole; knowing that is true humility. The only greatness we have is being part of the body of Christ and learning from him meekness and humility" (p. 169). She echoes St. Paul, who experienced a "thorn in the flesh" that kept him from being conceited. He boasted of his weaknesses and learned to rely on the power of God. (2 Cor. 12: 7-10) This pandemic is our thorn in the flesh, teaching us to rely on God's power in our lives.

Joy: We imagine that suffering can only bring us misery. It leads to the despair of no escape. However, Christ's passion shows another side of suffering. As an act of loving self-sacrifice it brings untold joy.

Houselander affirmed, "In real sacrifice, there is joy which surpasses all other joys, it is the crescendo and culmination of love." (p. 10) Chasing after pleasure will eventually turn to pain. We can never get enough. However, sacrificing ourselves out of love, as Jesus did, brings lasting joy and new life. Only love lasts, along with the joy that accompanies it.

Compassion: Suffering can either close our hearts in self-pity or open them in compassion. Our suffering creates a bond with everyone on the planet. The passion teaches us that Christ is revealed in all those we meet who are wounded. Houselander, who firmly believed in Christ's presence in all, especially in the least of our brothers and sisters, wrote, "We cannot see Christ in his glory, but we can see him and touch him in man's suffering. Our contemplation in the world is the contemplation of the humiliated Christ in mankind. Humanity is the veil of Veronica. It is, so to speak, the suffering Face of Christ on the Via Crucis." (p. 148) If we want to know Christ, we need to look closely at the faces of those who are suffering, bearing the imprints of his wounds.

Forgiveness: Our anger holds us hostage. We cling to it because it gives us the illusion of power. In reality, it is a poison that drains the life out of us. As Jesus was dying on the cross, he prayed, "Father, forgive them, for they know not what they do." Houselander affirmed the importance of taking on the mind and heart of Christ in the midst of a cruel war. She insisted that we must give up our hatred of the enemy who slaughters the innocent. Jesus taught that the highest form of love is love of our enemy, of those who do not deserve our love. He reminded us that God loves us as sinners. On the cross, he died for us as sinners. In the Lord's Prayer, we ask that God forgive us to the extent that we forgive others.

Redemption: We think of our suffering as a punishment for our wrongdoing. It is karma, the consequences of our actions. Houselander believed that Christ's passion reversed the normal meaning of suffering. She wrote, "When Christ became man, he uplifted man's nature together with all its vial activities. He changed man's suffering into his passion. Man's suffering became redemptive….Through Christ, suffering has become, not an evil to be avoided at all costs, but a thing to be accepted willingly, even joyfully, as a means of sharing in the redemption of the world." (p. 145, 147) The resurrection reveals that new life comes from suffering and death. If we embrace our suffering as an offering of love, we participate in God's work to redeem the world.

As we struggle through the pandemic and its aftermath, we search to uncover its meaning for ourselves. We look for some image that will guide us in our healing and recovery. Two eccentric mystics, Caryll Houselander and Julian of Norwich, believed that all our suffering is a sharing in the passion of Christ. We do not suffer alone. Christ dwells within us all, especially in our woundedness. He assures us that if we die with him, sacrificing ourselves in love, we will also rise with him. Embracing the tribulations of the pandemic can lead to the redemption of our world.

CHAPTER TWELVE

GOOD GRIEF

"But who weeps for God? Cry to Him with a real cry."
—Sri Ramakrishna

We Catholics live with hope because we believe in the resurrection of the body and life everlasting.

Sadness at the untold losses caused by the pandemic will long outlive the Coronavirus. At this writing, a majority of Americans have been infected, and millions suffer long-term effects. There have been over one million deaths. Many have been hospitalized and died separated from family and friends. The losses of loved ones, health, financial and job security, lifestyle, and precious times together have been staggering. The emotional trauma of the pandemic will make a permanent mark on this generation. In fact, current research indicates that nearly a third of both adults and children now suffer from clinical levels of depression and anxiety.

In therapy sessions, I accompany my patients as they work with their fears and grief. During the months of this global tragedy, I have written essays to give voice to my own suffering and struggle to make sense of it. A friend of mine has been writing poetry this past year. The image of an abandoned car wreck inspired her to write a poem on sorrow that touched a wellspring of buried pain within her. She observed a common thread through her poems—heartache.

Many of us reflect and journal to cope. A recent poem by a retired Wisconsin teacher, Kitty O'Meara, went viral on the Internet and captured the imagination of the American public. It was presented as written in 1869 and reprinted during the Spanish flu of 1919. She wrote: "The earth also began to heal/And when the danger ended and/People found themselves/They grieved for the dead/and made new choices/And dreamed of new visions/And created new ways of living/And completely healed the earth/ Just as they were healed." (March, 2020)

For many, this pandemic has been a long inconvenience without significant loss. For many others, though, the sadness at this time is overwhelming and even debilitating. How can we pass through this vale of tears and survive? How can we grieve well? What new life can emerge from our sorrows?

GRIEF STRICKEN

Many of us are grief stricken and stuck. We have suffered so many losses and do not know how to negotiate the labyrinth of our sorrow. We have lost our way. The classic book by Elizabeth Kubler-Ross, *On Death and Dying* (1), outlined five stages of grief. She observed that grieving is a process that takes time and circles back upon itself. We can easily become stuck in one of the stages of the process as we struggle to move toward the acceptance of the loss.

Denial: We numb ourselves to cope with the pain of loss. We can use alcohol, drugs, or distracting activity to distance ourselves from unpleasant feelings. The strategy works and may be needed for temporary relief. However, such denial comes at a price. When we shut out the pain, we also cut out the joy. All the emotions that enliven us are deadened. Further, when unwanted feelings are suppressed, they do not simply disappear. They go underground to grow as seeds in our fertile unconscious. They grow secretly in strength, influencing our moods and behaviors in unsuspected ways. One day they flower in distressful psychological symptoms, which are the return of the repressed.

Anger: We protest what was taken away from us against our wills. "That should not be!" we lament. Perhaps we envisioned a world without ever losing what we love most. Now we suffer disillusionment and sense of powerlessness. Our rage serves a purpose. It protects us for a while from an overwhelming sense of helplessness. It keeps us from falling into the abyss of despair. Anger gives us the illusion of power when we feel so weak. However, if the anger becomes chronic as a defense against sadness, it will eventually consume us. A slogan of Alcoholics Anonymous alerts us, "Nurturing anger is like consuming rat poison and expecting the rat to die." We do not regain what was lost but die emotionally from the poison.

Bargaining: In the throes of grieving, we inevitably review the past. We examine what happened and how we could have prevented the loss. "If only I had done something differently, this would not have happened. If only I had been vaccinated…" The anger we feel toward the universe, or fate, that caused our suffering slowly becomes directed against ourselves. Guilt consumes us. We may even bargain with God to take away our pain. The self-blame and bargaining serve a purpose. When we are feeling so out of control of our lives, we create the illusion of mastery. We imagine we could have done something to prevent the loss.

Depression: When we are stuck in sorrow, we become depressed. The mood becomes like a drug, a tranquilizer that makes us sleepwalk through life. We have no energy or motivation to engage actively in life. We become zombies. We do not believe we can survive without what we lost. Such temporary withdrawal serves a purpose. It enables us to stop, look, and listen to ourselves to nurse our wounds. However, if the sleepwalking becomes a way of life, we die inside. We feel helpless and hopeless. Tragically, we may fall into despair or choose suicide to escape the pain.

Anxiety: I add another stage to Kubler-Ross' list—anxiety. Anxiety is the constant companion of depression. Both are a reaction to loss. When we are depressed, we mourn past losses. Our ruminating makes us prisoners of our past wounds. When we suffer anxiety, we worry about future losses. We imagine catastrophes and create a nightmare fantasy world. Anxiety also serves a survival purpose. It alerts us to possible danger and motivates us to take protective actions. However, if the anxiety becomes excessive, it becomes like a drug. It is like a stimulant that keeps us aroused and unable to focus on the present moment.

The final stage of grief is embracing the wisdom of acceptance and freedom.

GOOD GRIEF

When grief takes over our lives, we are its slave. Sorrow rules us. We refuse to accept the reality of the losses suffered and live in bondage to our illusions. We long for a world without suffering. We protest what has been taken from us against our will. We desire complete control of our lives. However, the way out of our distress is to give up our futile resistance and wisely accept the reality of the loss. We imagine that we cannot be happy without what and whom we hold dear. But is that really true? Only embracing the truth and surrendering our illusions will set us free. There are several steps on the path to freedom:

Gift of Tears: We accept our suffering. Instead of fleeing our sadness, we embrace it wholeheartedly. The Buddha instructed his followers on the first noble truth: "Life is suffering, heartbreak." He observed that we continually get what we do not want and do not get what we want. Over and over, our powerlessness over life assaults us. We resist, and our suffering increases. Jesus preached the same message to his disciples. They objected when he told them that he had to suffer and die. Jesus rebuked them and said, "If anyone wishes to come after me, he must deny his very self, take up his cross, and begin to follow in my footsteps. Whoever would save his life will lose it, but whoever loses his life for my sake will find it." (Matt. 16: 24-25)

We spontaneously give voice to our sorrow to be heard and healed. The Psalmist prayed, "Out of the depths I cry to you, O Lord; Lord, hear my voice! Let your ears be attentive to my voice in supplication." (Psalm 130: 1-2) His prayer inspired confidence in God's mercy. His tears cleansed his soul. God's heart melts like that of a mother who hears her baby cry out in pain.

Our heartache touches our deepest self and God.

Tender Heart: We accept that we are not alone in our suffering. The heart can be a lonely hunter. Self-pity can isolate us. Our sorrows can harden our hearts if our woundedness becomes our identity. However, our broken heart may also open us to the suffering of the world. Holding the pain can make our hearts tender, compassionate to the suffering of others. We are all in this together. We are one body and share the sorrows of our neighbors next door and across the world. Our shared suffering and our mutual efforts to relieve it can unite us.

Our sorrow connects us with others.

Truth of Impermanence: We accept our loss as part of life. We observe that loss, dying, and rising are built into the fabric of the universe. The seasons come and go and return again. There is no new life unless there is death. That is the cycle of life. We are the universe's offspring. Our bodies are in constant change, in continual interchange with the environment as we age. We come from the earth and eventually return to it. Even our thoughts and feelings are in constant flux, not permanent. They pass like clouds in the brilliant blue sky of our consciousness.

Jesus reminded us that we have no lasting dwelling place in this world and said, "In my Father's house there are many dwelling places; otherwise, how could I have told you that I was going to prepare a place for you?" (John 14: 2) If we cling to a piece of this earth, we will only be disappointed and increase our misery. However, if we accept the passing nature of our lives, we will be free. A Buddhist saying expresses this wisdom: "All things are impermanent./They arise and they pass away./ To live in harmony with this truth/Brings great happiness."

Our sadness puts us in harmony with the universe.

Loss and Longing: What we grieve for expresses what we hold dear. Our sorrow reveals our lost love, our heart's treasure. When we are overcome with sadness, we can examine closely our longings: "What am I missing so much? What makes it so important to me? Does my happiness depend on possessing what I lost?"

Grief also presents an opportunity to ask ourselves a more probing question: "Are my desires deep enough and large enough?" Ramakrishna, the Indian sage and saint, inquired, "Who weeps for God? People shed a whole jug of tears for wife and children. They swim in tears for money. But who weeps for God? Cry to Him with a real cry." (2)

St. Therese of Lisieux, the little flower, had a sensitive soul. She suffered greatly because of her exquisite sensitivity and often shed tears. She wrote in her autobiography, "The tears and blood of Jesus were to be her dew, and her Sun was His adorable face veiled with tears. Until I came to Carmel, I had never fathomed the depths of the treasures hidden in his Holy Face." (3) Therese found consolation by joining her sorrows with those of Jesus who shed his blood and tears for the whole world.

Our grief expands our consciousness and increases our wisdom.

HIBERNATE

In the grip of mourning, we hibernate. We are drained of energy and motivation and want to withdraw from our normal activities. We back off to nurse our wounds. The pandemic has interrupted our usual routines and forced us to spend time alone with ourselves. The quiet and stillness has been difficult for many of us. However, it is also an opportunity to enter deeply into our sadness and heal.

Kitty O'Meara suggested a way through the grief during the pandemic. She wrote: "And people stayed/And read books/And listened/ And they rested/And did exercises/And made art and played/And stopped and listened/More deeply/Someone meditated, someone prayed/Someone met their shadow/And people began to think differently/And people healed."

Our grieving will bear fruit if we allow ourselves to sit with our sorrows. Just sit in silence with our sadness to see what emerges. Every impulse within us wants to run away from the pain by falling asleep. We will heal and bring forth new life from the pain if we let it be our teacher. We need to feel deeply our sadness and listen to the message it offers. Some life force within us is crying out to be released. We need to be awake and aware of the deeper longings hidden in the sadness. Entering the dark cave of our sorrow we will discover a buried treasure. We may be surprised at our resilience, resourcefulness, and longings for a more abundant life.

Facing the inevitable tragedies of life, we throw up our arms and exclaim, "Good grief!" That is both our complaint and hope. We have suffered the loss of so many loved ones, our health, our economic security, and our way of life. We mourn these terrible losses. The sadness may crush us. Or it may enliven us. Our tears can be cleansing. If we grieve wisely and well, we can surrender our illusions and distorted desires. Then, a new life beyond our imagining may flower from the fertile ground of our sorrow.

CHAPTER THIRTEEN

GOD'S GAME OF LIFE

"This world is the Lila (playground) of God. It is like a game."
—Sri Ramakrishna

We Catholics believe in the Wisdom of God revealed in Jesus Christ. Wisdom was present from the beginning "playing on the surface of his earth and finding delight in the human race." (Proverbs 8: 31) Wisdom shows her face in unexpected places.

Pleasure teaches us nothing. We simply enjoy it and wish it would last forever. In contrast, pain is the great teacher. While suffering, we wonder about the cause, how we can survive, and how we can end it. We long for the return of pleasure. Pain also provokes the inner journey of exploration. We try to make sense of it so we can find relief.

The pandemic has been a painful time for all of us. We have struggled through it, wishing for its end. Meanwhile, we try to make sense of what is happening to us on a worldwide scale. Scientists are unlocking the mysterious DNA of the Coronavirus and finding protections and cures. We try to cope emotionally and mentally with the disruption caused by the pandemic as best we can. "How can we survive and maintain our lifestyles?" we ask ourselves.

If we allow ourselves to explore the meaning of the pandemic to its depths, we naturally ask the question, "Where is God in all this?" This crisis provides an opportunity to examine our religious worldviews. We ask these questions with a deadly seriousness. Our wellbeing and happiness depend on the answers we discover.

Our images of God affect where we locate His Presence in this time of suffering. Where we find God and how we understand Him influence our attitudes toward life and our coping styles.

GOD AS CRITICAL SPECTATOR

We Americans think very differently about God. In her book *Christianity After Religion (1)*, Diana Butler Bass documents the monumental belief and practice changes Americans are undergoing at the present time. Since our founding, we have been a proudly Christian nation. In 2008, the Pew Research Center conducted a thorough and widespread poll of the American people, interviewing 35,000. They observed that since 1960 the number of Americans claiming belief in God went from "most emphatic" at 97% to 71%. A large proportion, nearly 20%, claimed no religious affiliation; nearly a third of those under 30 years of age were unaffiliated. (p. 46) Still, 92% reported some belief in the Divine.

The researchers asked believers about their images of God. Of adults, 60% claimed that God was a person "with whom people can have a relationship," while 25% defined God as an impersonal force. Seven percent related that it was impossible to know anything about God. The Baylor University researchers discovered that among the 92% who believe in God, many believed in very different Gods. The largest group was those who had faith in an Authoritarian God (31%), who is a wrathful, sin-hating deity. The next largest group composed those who believe in a Distant God (24%). Their God is the cosmic creative force behind and beyond the natural universe. Sixteen percent put their faith in a Critical God who would bring justice in the end. The final group accepted a Benevolent God (23%) who is the forgiving friend of sinners and a caring healer. (pp. 49-50)

These data indicate that the vast majority of Americans today view God as a Critical Spectator. Consequently, we experience God as standing back and judging us in and through the pandemic. COVID-19 is somehow God's judgment on us for our failings, past and present. God is also watching how we respond. He will reward or punish us according to our response. Instead of feeling comforted, we live in fear through this ordeal if we see God as a harsh Judge.

Such a merciless view of God's attitude toward our suffering has deep roots within our Western tradition. For example, Jonathan Edwards, a well-known colonial theologian, preached a sermon which captured the religious thinking of an age preoccupied with Puritanical guilt. It was entitled, "Sinners in the Hands of an Angry God." He threatened hell fire for those not living up to the ideals of the Gospel. A few years before, England was being ravaged by the Black Plague. Daniel Defoe wrote in his journal of the plague that pastors interpreted it as an act of God's retribution for our sins. More recently, Billy Graham, the noted American evangelist, claimed that the HIV/AIDS epidemic was God's punishment for homosexuals. Today, many religious-minded are inclined to view COVID-19 as God's reprimand for abortions, racism, the neglect of the poor, the exploitation of our environment, and so forth.

LIFE AS A COURTROOM

How we view God bleeds into how we see life. If God is our Judge and Law-Maker, our life is a courtroom. In a courtroom, people play many different roles. In this scenario, we identify most with the role of defendant. We are accused of doing something wrong and stand trial. We live in the defensive mode to avoid punishment. An advocate supports our cause. The prosecutor presents a case against us, exposing our violations of the law. He assumes the role of our persecutor and enemy. The jury of our peers watches us closely, evaluates us, and renders a judgment. We feel like we are under the microscope of their judgment, careful not to make any misstep. The judge oversees the whole process, eventually declares us guilty or not, and then sentences us.

Standing trial naturally evokes fear and dread. However, if we live our daily lives as if we are in a courtroom, the fear and dread never leave us. The joy is drained from our lives. In our imaginary courtroom, we feel victimized by a cruel world. We grumble about our fate and the unfairness of life. We see ourselves as helpless victims surrounded by persecutors. Preoccupied with our sinfulness, we feel guilty and await punishment. That punishment may come in many forms: lost jobs, poor health, broken relationships, and even an unwanted pandemic. Self-conscious of our inadequacies, everyone is a member of a jury who is judging us. God is the judge, not an advocate, who will make the final and fatal condemnation for our unworthiness.

Conventional, fear-based religion promotes resignation and despair during tough times. There is little good news, joy, or hope, as Jesus proclaimed.

GOD AS PLAYFUL PARTICIPANT

The Eastern tradition presents an alternative view of God's involvement in the world. From a Hindu perspective, God is actively involved in creating, preserving, and destroying the universe in ongoing cycles of death and rebirth. God, called Brahman, is eternal and unchanging. Brahman creates the universe as Its playground through Sakti (also called Kali) who is Its dynamic presence. Brahman is the Ultimate Reality that manifests Itself in the world of appearances, called Maya.

The world we experience is ever-changing, impermanent, and lacking any real substance. However, God resides everywhere and in everyone. The Divine Presence in humans is called Atman, which represents the changeless core of our identity in this constantly shifting universe.

God spontaneously created the universe, a playground in which all beings are actively engaged. Brahman created the universe out of Bliss, for Bliss. The earth is the Divine Mother, who displays both the beauty and savagery of nature. She is the Primordial Energy that drives life. We actively engage in this Divine Drama, called Lila. Sri Ramakrishna, the Indian saint and sage, taught, "This world is the Lila of God. It is like a game. In this game there are joy and sorrow, virtue and vice, knowledge and ignorance, good and evil. The game cannot continue if sin and suffering are altogether eliminated from creation." (2)

God plays a game of hide-and-seek with us. The world both conceals and reveals its Divine Ground. We struggle to overcome our ignorance. We gain glimpses of God's Presence in coming to know our true nature as His children. In this game, we are seduced by worldly desires to cling to the world of appearances. Self-renunciation and discrimination are required to discern what is truly Real and lasting, God's Presence. In knowing God, we come to know ourselves and achieve everlasting joy.

LIFE AS A GYMNASIUM

If God created the world spontaneously for sport, our life is a gymnasium, playground, sport field. Any sport requires opponents, rules, and a goal. We welcome worthy opponents to prove and improve our skills. We train diligently for the contest, realizing there is no gain without pain. When the match begins, we agree to a set of rules that limits the game. Both sides keep their eyes on the goal. We compete whole-heartedly, to the best of our ability, to defeat our opponent and achieve the prize. In the process, we gain confidence, respect for others, and a sense of satisfaction. We know full well that how we play the game is always more important than the outcome. We are all winners if we compete with integrity.

In the same way, this Divine Drama of life requires competing characters, opposition, and worthy adversaries. The tension of opposites is built into the fabric of the universe. As much as we hate conflict, we know that without it life is dull and meaningless. Trials and conflict are unavoidable. They often come in unwanted, painful, and inconvenient ways, such as this pandemic. Inevitably, the pain of loss, sickness, and death will strike us all.

We may grumble about the game as unfair. Or we may see the Presence of God at play and embrace the challenge. God is working through us as we compete against the troublemakers within and outside us. Our trials and tribulations are like exercise machines that, when used properly, enable us to grow in strength and endurance. In this game of life, adversity provides the opportunity for us to develop character. Something new always emerges from the struggle. Our problems cannot touch the core of who we are. However, how we compete against our opponents proves our true worth as human beings. In the end, we are assured that the goal of life's competition is joy.

Recognizing God's abiding Presence enables us to face life's challenges with courage, joy, and hope.

GOOD SPORTSMANSHIP

If we view life as God's game in which He is intimately involved, good sportsmanship naturally motivates us. In fact, God is so invested in the game that He dwells within all of us. St. Paul asked, "Do you not know that you are a temple of God and that the Spirit of God dwells in you?" (I Cor. 3:16) God is not a distant, critical Spectator. He is on the playing field with us. The following are some qualities for playing the game of life wisely and well:

<u>Be supportive.</u> The game of life is a team sport. We are all in this together. Unlike conventional religion that tends to make salvation an individual affair, God's intimate involvement with all of us makes our life on this planet a team effort. Instead of criticizing our fellow athletes, we encourage them to give their best performance. We win or lose as a team, not as isolated individuals. In our competition, we bring out the best in each of us.

<u>Be respectful.</u> Since God dwells in all of us, everyone deserves respect. That includes our opponents and all those who make our lives challenging. Even our so-called enemies deserve our respect. We are all equally children of God. Sri Ramakrishna commented, "One attains Perfect Knowledge when one sees God in man. Now I see that it is God alone who is moving about in various forms: as a holy man, as a cheat, as a villain." (p. 419)

<u>Have fun.</u> The purpose of this game of life is to have fun, to enjoy it. This fun is not amusement park fun, but a light-hearted joy that does not take ourselves too seriously. It is confidence that, no matter what happens in life. "All will be well, every kind of thing will be well," Julian of Norwich affirms. Happiness is our birthright.

Many religious-minded who live under the scrutiny of a judging God take themselves and their lives too seriously. They live in fear under the shadow of divine judgment. The world for them is a "vale of tears." However, we cannot forget that God spontaneously created the universe for sport so we could share His Bliss. That is also the message of the Gospel, the good news, that Jesus proclaimed. We can play freely and light-heartedly like children because we trust our Divine Parent.

<u>Commit to fair play.</u> We can have fun in the game of life if we have the security of established rules for fairness. We are all born equal and deserve a level playing field. Our opponents are not our enemies whom we defeat to build ourselves up. This is a friendly competition. The game cannot be enjoyable and rewarding unless there is justice in our

world. Justice demands that we share our resources so all have their basic needs met.

Have a positive attitude. In this game of life, we welcome all the challenges that come our way. We consider all the troubles we face as opportunities for growth. We also have confidence in facing our difficulties because we know that God dwells within us and works through us. His strength overcomes our weaknesses. Nothing can ultimately defeat us or touch the core of who we are as God's children. St. Paul asked, "If God is for us, who can be against us?...Who will separate us from the love of Christ? Trial, or distress, or persecution, or hunger, or nakedness, or danger, or the sword?" (Rom. 8: 31, 35)

Be willing to learn. We cannot realistically expect to win every game we play. We cannot expect never to make a mistake. Failures and errors, sometimes major ones, will inevitably occur. We may succumb to feelings of hopelessness, give in to guilt, and throw in the towel. Or we can pick ourselves up and keep trying. It takes courage and humility to learn from our mistakes and keep playing the game. In the end, we learn more from our defeats than our successes.

Accept responsibility. When we face worthy opponents in life, we may complain about our bad luck. We may even blame others for our defeats. "If only...then, we would be winners," we tell ourselves. However, each of us has been given a role and task in life according to our abilities, temperaments, and interests. Our joy in life will be determined not by how often we win but by how we play the game. Playing wholeheartedly and with integrity, we can be equally gracious in victory and defeat.

Practice self-control. Our most challenging opponents are not those we meet on the playing field of life, but those within our own minds. Our worst troublemakers are our fears, selfish desires, and prejudices. Our temper outbursts can cause irreparable harm to ourselves and others. We will spend a lifetime confronting our inner demons, not letting them take over our lives. Through cultivating the angels of our better nature we can learn self-control.

Times of stress, such as the pandemic, provoke a deep questioning of our values and beliefs. For many of us, our image of God as a Critical Spectator and Judge offers little consolation. However, more meaningful and comforting views of God can help us cope with our suffering. Many others, especially those influenced by the Eastern Traditions, view God as intimately involved in our lives, as a loving and playful Participant in the universe. The world is the divine playground. God dwells within us all and works through us all in these trying times to discover His Presence and find Bliss. Our sportsmanlike conduct can sustain and enable us to grow in love for one another.

CHAPTER FOURTEEN

DON'T LOOK UP

"Then you will know the truth, and the truth will set you free."
—Jesus of Nazareth

We Catholics seek to know the fullness of Truth, wherever it may be found. In knowing Truth, we know God.

Art imitates life. I recently watched a controversial movie, "Don't Look Up," which had a star-studded cast: Leo DiCaprio, Meryl Streep, and Jennifer Lawrence. It is a disaster satire that is both funny and scary. A group of scientists discover a comet that is on a path to make a direct hit on earth. The comet is so large that the collision would destroy our planet. Scientists around the world try to warn the government and the public of the imminent destruction.

But the politicians, news media, and business leaders ignore them. They say, "Keep your head down. Don't look up." These groups are so focused on their own immediate interests that they ignore the impending danger. The politicians do not want to upset their constituency before the election. The news media desire to keep their audiences entertained and distracted. The businessmen try to figure out a way to make money mining the asteroid.

Adam McKay, the writer/director of the movie, reported that he wrote the story as a metaphor for climate change. Scientists express dire warnings about the horrific consequences of global warming. The public and its leaders cannot come to agreement for concerted action to avert the disaster. Many do not believe it is real. McKay implores us to wake up before it is too late.

The movie highlights starkly different ways of thinking to address a crisis. Some, represented by the scientists, tell everyone to look up and see the reality of what is happening. Others are so focused on fulfilling their immediate needs that they ignore reality. Like Nero, they play their fiddles while Rome burns.

The movie can also be a metaphor for our handling any crisis, such as the pandemic. Our thinking becomes polarized. The global crisis of the pandemic has revealed our differing ways of thinking about the event. The approaches are so different that we are often experience a stalemate over how to care for ourselves and one another. How much of a threat is COVID-19? Which is more dangerous: COVID-19 or the vaccine? Do we really need to be vaccinated, wear masks, social distance, and quarantine? Is our proposed cure in shutting down the economy and closing schools worse than the disease?

With such divergent ways of thinking, how can we communicate with one another? How can we understand each other and reach compromises?

UNLIKE OUTLOOKS

Freud provides a useful framework for understanding our divergent ways of thinking. In analyzing his dreams, he discovered how the mind works. Freud observed two distinct patterns of mental functioning, one older and more primitive, the other newer and more mature. He identified the more primitive as primary process functioning, which is governed by the pleasure principle. The mind is need-driven to seek pleasure and avoid pain. Self-interest motivates it. It seeks immediate gratification and cannot tolerate the frustration of delay: "I want it all, and I want it now!" Infants react to their environment with primary process thinking. They often engage in fantasy and magical thinking to get their needs met.

As we mature and adjust through the struggles of life, our thinking also adapts. Freud called the more mature thinking style secondary process functioning in which the reality principle predominates. The more mature mind is able to delay gratification of its needs for future greater satisfactions. It is able to assess situations, consider options, and weigh their consequences. Evidence gathering and reasoning shape the choices made. As we mature, we tend to respond consciously to our environment and react less automatically.

We all engage in both primary and secondary process thinking, but in different measures. In times of stress, we may feel overwhelmed and unable to think through objectively what needs to be done. In those moments, we regress to more childlike, automatic ways of reacting.

LOOKING IN DIFFERENT DIRECTIONS

During the pandemic, many of us have experienced enormous stress, which may affect our thinking and decision-making. Some measure of fear is inescapable with the threat of COVID-19 to our physical, emotional, and social wellbeing. In my practice as a clinical psychologist, I observe how anxiety shapes the way my patients' adjust to life. I try to help them think clearly and make rational decisions in their best interest. In other words, I invite them to engage in secondary process thinking, to trust their wise minds.

For example, in deciding whether or not to be vaccinated, I observe two distinct styles of thinking:

On the one hand, those of us who have decided to be vaccinated listen to science. We want everybody to be vaccinated for the safety of the planet. We are not scientists or experts on the pandemic. So, we look to some authority for guidance. Where do we look?

Science becomes our trusted guide. Science represents secondary process thinking. It is rational and systematic. Scientists around the world observed carefully the beginning, spread, and evolution of COVID-19. They shouted, "Look at what's happening; don't look up with your heads in the clouds!" They alerted the world to a life-threatening danger. Using a stringent scientific method, they gathered data, analyzed the results of controlled studies, and wrote up their conclusions. Their method offered probable, not certain, answer to medical questions.

Further, these scientists presented their work to the whole scientific community for peer review. Official agencies, such as the World Health Organization, the Center for Disease Control, and the Federal Drug Administration, then reviewed available studies about the Coronavirus, vaccines, treatments, and the benefits of wearing masks and social distancing. On the basis of their ongoing reviews, they make recommendations for our public health.

On the other hand, those of us who object to being vaccinated follow a different mental protocol. We value our personal research and freedom to decide what is best for us. We believe that the vaccine is more dangerous than COVID-19. How do we come to this conclusion?

We engage in primary process thinking, though not all would agree with this assessment. The news about the deadliness and unpredictability of COVID-19 may terrify us. So, we turn away from the harsh reality reported by the scientists because we find it so unbearable. "Keep your head down; don't look up," we tell ourselves, without knowing it. We question the validity of the scientific evidence and dispute it with a vengeance.

We find refuge in an alternative view of reality that we find more comfortable. Magical thinking that the pandemic will just disappear comforts us. We believe that the pandemic is not really as serious as the government, scientists, or the media make it out to be. Instead, we see the vaccine as more dangerous and resent mandates to impose it on us.

What we have done is displace our fear of COVID-19 onto the vaccine. We cannot control the disease, but we can control what medicines enter our bodies. "My body, my choice!" we exclaim. We also object to any inconveniences, such as mask-wearing and social distancing. To justify our belief, we look to random experts, studies, and anecdotal reports on the Internet. Feedback from like-minded friends reinforces our biases and makes us feel more secure in our opinions.

Our fear intensifies and spreads into a paranoid mindset for some of us. We are alert for possible enemies, someone to blame for our misery. We do not trust the government, the media, or the scientists. Some of us call them "the unholy trinity: big government, big media, and big Pharma." Their representatives are President Biden, Bill Gates, and Anthony Fauci. We accuse these groups of stealing our lifestyle and freedom for their own selfish purposes. We find signs of a hidden conspiracy behind their promotion of the vaccine. We pursue the grandiose mission of being vigilant guardians of society against abuse by the establishment. Our mistrust of conventional authority leads us to seek alternative, dissenting sources of information in social media.

Because of the differences in thinking styles, open discussions about the vaccine become challenging. Opposing views divide families, friends, and the nation. These conversations often become hostile. So, we avoid them. Resentment brews against those of differing opinions whom we believe are causing great harm. Accusations abound. "The unvaccinated prolong the pandemic," some say. Others claim, "The vaccinated try to force us to take a dangerous drug against our will."

How can we break the stalemate? How can we engage in an authentic dialogue?

LOOKING AHEAD TOGETHER

Even though we may disagree with the opinions and ways of thinking of each other, we share more in common than we realize. We all engage in both primary and secondary process thinking in different measures at different times. We are all preoccupied with satisfying our needs, seeking pleasure, and avoiding pain. There are moments, however, when we all regress to less mature thought processes, especially under duress. Then, self-protection becomes paramount. Often disagreements on important issues arouse in us intense emotions which interfere with our clear thinking and communicating. Fear drives us to keep our heads down and not look up. Nevertheless, we still possess a wise, mature mind that is reasonable in pursuing higher values.

Mark Ortman, a teacher and writer on communication, wrote a useful book that provides guidance in how to talk without arguing when we face strong disagreement. (1) He proposed a 3-stage model of communication, which he calls the A.C.T. way: acknowledge, clarify, talk.

Acknowledge

In the first stage, we listen carefully to the speaker's interests, emotions, values, and needs behind their words. We attune to the importance the speaker gives to the issue at hand. We then acknowledge the speaker's experience to create an atmosphere conducive to mutual understanding when emotions are present. Strong emotions can compromise our ability to listen, reason, and speak clearly. We are stuck if we cannot move beyond self-interested primary process thinking.

The vaccine debate arouses intense emotions. Both sides are fearful. We fear either the dangers of the vaccine or of COVID-19. We are also angry because of the stalemate in the debate, which threatens our security. We may be angry that the unvaccinated prolong the pandemic by their stubborn refusal to listen to the voice of science, the voice of reason. Or we may resent the pressure to take a medicine we believe dangerous to our wellbeing.

We can help defuse the emotional volatility of the debate by acknowledging the fear and anger that hold us captive. We can replace them with compassion for ourselves and our opponents. Further, we can go deeper by recognizing the differing values that underlie our points of view. We share a mutual need for safety, health, and self-preservation. At the same time, though, we can attest to our differing views of personal freedom and the common good.

Clarify

Next, we try to clarify what the speaker means and wants by asking pertinent questions. Our sincere curiosity, without judgment, shows our interest and respect for the speaker's point of view. No one possesses the full truth. A full pot can hold nothing new. As my mentor often said, "Much of what we hear are half-truths. When we hear a half-truth, look for the other half!" Before sharing our half, we try to understand the speaker's half first.

The vaccine debate revolves around two questions. First, which is more dangerous: COVID-19 or the vaccine? Second, what authority do we trust? Since we are not scientists, we look to other experts to help us make up our minds. To whom do we turn?

Those of us who view COVID-19 as dangerous and the vaccine as safe listen to the consensus of scientific opinion. We can ask those who disagree with us to help us understand their point of view. How is the vaccine dangerous? What led you to this conclusion? What is the evidence? What are your sources? How do you know they are reliable?

How do you know you can trust them more than the opinion of the scientific community? What do you make of the consensus of scientific opinion about the safety and effectiveness of the vaccines? How dangerous do you see COVID-19 to our health and wellbeing? Do you have an alternative suggestion for protection and safety? What is the evidence of its effectiveness as a replacement for the vaccine?

Those of us who view the vaccines as dangerous dispute the current conventional wisdom. We can ask those who disagree with us how they came to their conclusion? What is the evidence? What convinces you personally that COVID-19 is so dangerous and the vaccine so safe and effective? What do you think about the publicized negative side effects of the vaccine? How do you know you can trust the scientific reports? Do you believe the scientists looked at all the available evidence? How do you know there are not other more effective safeguards than medication?

Asking these questions with genuine curiosity and listening with an open mind can prime the pump for a genuine dialogue.

Talk

Finally, we explain our point of view. We state as clearly as we can what we know and want, why it is important to us, and how we can act on our insights. The clear expression of our ideas invites the listener to expand his own viewpoint. In short, this method engages us in reasonable secondary process thinking to resolve conflicts and reach agreements.

The questions of those who oppose our point of view can stimulate us to look more deeply into our own convictions. Those questions suggest what our opponents think and consider important. Our dialogue is built on our common interest in good health and protection from the disease. In that light, we explain as clearly as we can what we believe, why it is important, and how we can achieve our mutual goal of global wellbeing.

Through that dialogue we may learn from those who oppose vaccines the anomalies about the effects of the vaccine that need further investigation. We may also learn alternative ways of protection and treatment for COVID-19, such as a better diet, exercise, vitamin supplements. Alternative medicine approaches may complement and enhance traditional medical treatments.

By the same token, we may learn from vaccine advocates a larger perspective from the results of scientific investigation. Science presents us with a big picture based on a large-scale gathering of data, expert analysis, and a review of the results by the whole scientific community. Science makes powerful claims of rational objectivity by following a stringent method and code. Listening to science, we can learn more about the dangers of COVID-19 and the costs/benefits of using vaccines.

The pandemic has caused a crisis which has divided our nation and exposed our differing ways of viewing important matters. Fear cripples our clear thinking. Our biased views imprison us, stalemating open dialogue. Nevertheless, we fight the pandemic together and desire a healthy society. We also have wise minds that can navigate the obstacle-strewn path toward solutions. Looking straight ahead together, guided by our common interests, we can reach our goal of renewed health.

CHAPTER FIFTEEN

GOD'S SONG

"Music is a higher revelation than all wisdom and philosophy."
—Ludwig van Beethoven

We Catholics believe in the Holy Spirit, the divine energy of life, love, and truth. No institution can contain it.

John, a middle-aged patient of mine, suddenly developed tinnitus, a ringing in his ears. It happened suddenly when he was working on a job in a small room. He heard a loud crashing sound, and then the ringing began. Instead of getting better, it worsened every day. John suspected his bout with COVID-19 had something to do with it, but the doctors would not confirm that. They examined him and could find no structural damage to his inner ear. They offered few answers and little remedy. John complained to me, "I can't stand the roaring in my ears. I can't concentrate, hear clearly, or sleep at night. I'm so depressed and worried that the noise will not go away."

John loves music and even built a career around it, selling and installing audio-visual equipment. The loss of his hearing has been devastating. The constant mental noise distracts him from enjoying his everyday life. His preoccupation with his condition isolates him. He is terrified of becoming deaf. Now he struggles to release the mental uproar and again listen to the music of life.

John's condition exemplifies the way many of us choose to live. We live distracted lives. We keep ourselves busy with many concerns, all the things we believe need to be done. Our minds are always engaged, like wild monkey minds, with a pandemonium of thoughts. Our ceaseless thinking and planning often interfere with our sleep. "I'm not going to settle for a mediocre life; I'm not going to miss out on anything," we tell ourselves. "I'll rest when I'm dead," we add. There is always more to do to make our lives better—and so little time for peace and quiet.

Without realizing it, our frenetic activity deafens us. It makes us deaf to the music of the universe. Tragically, we are hardly aware of what we are missing.

GOD'S SONG

The major religious traditions proclaim that the universe is God's song.

A Hindu View

In the Hindu tradition, the *Bhagavad Gita* is the most sacred and revelatory text, like our Gospels. It relates the story of the divine Krishna guiding the warrior Arjuna in the midst of an internecine battlethat symbolizes the battlefield of life. Krishna reveals His own Divine nature, our human dignity, and the power of love. *Bhagavad Gita* translates into English as "The Song of God."

Paramahansa Yogananda, a Hindu teacher who brought the wisdom of the East to the West in the early 20th century, taught that the universe is God's cosmic song. He said that the Divine Spirit was alone and wanted to share His Bliss with others. So, a universe of the many, which has no beginning or end, is continually being created through cycles of birth, death, and rebirth. The Spirit pervades and manifests Himself in our world, singing His song. All creation is nothing but Spirit manifested in many forms, a variety of melodies.

Yogananda wrote in his commentary on the Christian Gospels:

> The Spirit was invisible, existing alone in the home of Infinity. He piped to Himself the ever-new, ever-entertaining song of perfect beatific Bliss. As He sang to Himself through His voice of Eternity, He wondered if aught but Himself were listening and enjoying His song. To His wittingly imposed astonishment, He felt His solitariness: He was the Cosmic Song, He was the Singing, and He was the Lone Enjoyer. Even as He thought, lo, He became two: Spirit and Nature, Man and Woman, Positive and Negative... (1)

The Cosmic Song brings joy and communion with our Creator and one another. It is a song we all sing in our hearts.

A Jewish View

The Hebrew Scriptures begin with the story of creation:

> In the beginning when God created the heavens and the earth, the earth was a formless wasteland and darkness covered the abyss, while a mighty wind swept over the waters. Then God said, 'Let there be light,' and there was light. God saw how good the light was. God then separated the light from the darkness. God called the light 'day,' and the darkness 'night.' Thus, evening came, and the morning followed—the first day. (Genesis 1: 1-5).

God spoke five more times and created the whole universe. On the sixth day, he created us humans in His own image and likeness. God then looked at everything he made and declared it very good. His word, the sound of His voice, created the universe. The divine voice reverberates everywhere.

King David was exquisitely attuned to God's voice and burst into song. God's word was music to his ears. David composed, sang, and danced to the music of the Psalms. In the Psalms he proclaimed the divine music of creation. The whole world inspired songs of praise. For example, in Psalm 8, he sang:

> How great is your name, O Lord our God,
>
> through all the earth!...
>
> When I see the heavens, the work of your hands,
>
> the moon and the stars which you arranged,
>
> what is man that you should keep him in mind,
>
> mortal man that you care for him?
>
> Yet you have made him little less than a god;
>
> with glory and honor you crowned him,
>
> gave him power over the works of your hand,
>
> put all things under his feet.

When he heard God's song in the world, David's heart was filled with joy. He burst into songs of praise, joy, and thanksgiving. He invited his followers to do the same. He chanted: "Cry out with joy to the Lord, all the earth./Serve the Lord with gladness./Come before him, singing for joy" (Psalm 100). For David, trust in God's goodness naturally expresses itself in a cheerful disposition. Everything is done gladly for the glory of God.

A Christian View

In the Christian tradition, Jesus came to proclaim the Gospel, which is the good news of the coming of God's kingdom. The first word of good news came with creation. John's Gospel begins:

In the beginning was the Word, and the Word was in God's presence, and the Word was God. He was present to God in the beginning. Through him all things came into being, and apart from him nothing came to be. Whatever came to be in him, found life, life for the light of men. The light shines on in darkness, a darkness that did not overcome it (John 1: 1-5).

In his commentary on this Gospel passage, Yogananda, reflecting the wisdom of the East, suggests we interpret *Word* as *sound* or *vibration*. It is movement created by energy. It is alive. The sound, however, is not chaotic and meaningless but rather expresses truth. It is a vibration shaped by intelligence. He said, "*Word* means intelligent vibration, intelligent energy, going forth from God…Likewise, the Word that is the beginning and source of all created substances is Cosmic Vibration imbued with Cosmic Intelligence (p. 9)." Yogananda calls the vibratory force, the creative life energy, emanating from Spirit the Holy Ghost. He labels the Cosmic Intelligence, the Divine Wisdom, that orders the chaos, the Christ Consciousness.

The universe hums with the Divine Presence, constantly moving, ordering, and creating anew. Those attuned to the full reality of our world hear the song of God's love. They respond with a joyous love for creation and all who dwell in it. Love inspires love. Hindus hear the holy Cosmic Sound as "Aum" or "Om," which embraces all our sounds. Other religious denominations respond to the sound of God's presence with "Amen!" Amen in Hebrew means "sure, faithful" and corresponds to the Oriental "Aum."

A Scientific View

Science today echoes the insights of our ancient religious traditions. Inspired by the theories of Albert Einstein, scientists have sought a unified field theory to describe nature's forces within a single, coherent framework. String theory is emerging as a possible explanatory framework. According to string theory, the "stuff" of all matter and energy is the same. The one fundamental ingredient in the universe is the string. The filaments that compose our material world vibrate in different patterns and frequencies, much like the strings of a musical instrument. Different patterns and frequencies of vibration produce different sounds, which scientists identify as elementary particles. These infinitesimal particles form into electrons, protons, and neutrons. Atoms combine into molecules and other increasingly complex forms. From this perspective, the universe is like a string symphony vibrating matter into existence. (2)

The universe is a dynamic balance of chaos and order. Creative life forces shape our world in unpredictable ways. Yet nature follows a mathematical pattern similar to music. Mathematical constants, such as pi, have been identified. We constantly attempt to refine our understanding of the laws of nature. To live a full life, we obviously need to attune ourselves to the underlying harmony of our often confusing world. We must honor both the uncharted movements of the Spirit and the guidance of intelligent decision-making.

How do we attune ourselves to God's song and the harmony of the universe?

SOUNDS OF SILENCE

Unfortunately, many of us get caught up in the cacophony of daily living. We hear the music of the universe only as loud noise that may grate on us. The clamor of hectic preoccupations and activities deafens us. Consequently, we experience much dissonance in our lives from competing desires and demands. There is little harmony, peace, or clear direction in our lives—no enrapturing melody.

Music is a mixture of sounds and silence. Notes are played with varying rhythms, tempos, and frequencies. Without intervening moments of silence, there is just noise, similar to the roaring in the ears that John experiences. In the same way, for us to hear and appreciate the music of the universe, we require both activity and quiet contemplation.

The subtle music of God's song of love can only be heard in silence, in solitude. We need to listen carefully and pay full attention, without distraction. We become absorbed in it, forgetting ourselves in the process. Like Elijah, who went into a cave to meet God, we listen for His Presence. Elijah did not encounter Him in the strong wind, the earthquake, or the blazing fire, but in the tiny whispering sound. (II Kings 19: 9-13) We too will hear the Divine Music as something soft and subtle, not loud and crashing.

Jesus recommended that we enter the privacy of our rooms and be still. He said, "Whenever you pray, go to your room, close your door, and pray to your Father in private. Then your Father, who sees what no man sees, will repay you. In your prayers, do not rattle on like the pagans. They think they will win a hearing by the sheer multiplication of words. Do not imitate them. Your Father knows what you need before you ask Him." (Matthew 6: 5-8) Jesus taught us to listen with open hearts and not be distracted by thoughts and words. Our reward will be that we will hear the song of His love.

Many today say, "I don't believe in God. So praying makes no sense." I respond, "If you take time to pray, to listen with an open mind and heart, you will sense God's Presence." We do not pray because we believe. Instead, we come to faith because we take the risk to pray. In the stillness we encounter Something or Someone greater than ourselves we cannot deny. If we are deafened by the clattering noise in our heads, we will never hear the sound of God's music.

Jesus promised a reward to those who pray in solitude. If we listen in silence to God's love song, our hearts will be filled with joy. We will hear the uplifting music in every circumstance of our lives. Even if we are frightened or sorrowful, even if we face overwhelming adversity, the music will sustain us. We can boast of our weaknesses and failings, confident of God's mercy and strength. We can face the tragedies of life with courage. As St. Paul exhorted, "Rejoice in the Lord always! I shall say it again: rejoice!" (Philippians 4: 4)

Good cheer is an infallible sign of authentic faith.

GOD'S INSTRUMENTS

Many believers give religion a bad name because of their sour dispositions. They view God as a harsh Judge or distant Critic. They practice their religion as if they are on trial, fearful of making a mistake and being punished. They see themselves as sinners begging for mercy. The universe is a courtroom. They are defendants.

In contrast, imagining the universe as the song of God can lift up our spirits. We feel raised to a higher level, absorbed into what transcends our everyday existence. If the universe is God's symphony, we are His instruments. King David chanted a psalm about praising God with a variety of instruments (Psalm 150):

"Praise God in his holy place…

O praise him with sound of trumpet,

praise him with lute and harp.

Praise him with timbrel and dance,

praise him with strings and pipes.

O praise him with resounding cymbals,

praise him with clashing of cymbals.

Let everything that lives and that breathes

give praise to the Lord."

God is the Conductor, we are the chosen instruments directed by Him to create a beautiful, harmonious melody. Our song is one of spontaneous praise. Each of us has a particular part to play in the orchestra that no one else can perform. Our life work is to discover that task, the uniqueness of the instrument and melody we must play. Our temperament, life experiences, abilities, and interests indicate the role God has assigned to us. By following the promptings of our true nature we come to know God's will for us. Then, our song will echo the Divine love song and create harmony in the world. In reality, God is the Musician and the music who plays through us. We will find our bliss only in performing our musical score according to the direction of the Divine Conductor.

We may experience unwanted stressful times, such as the pandemic, as a curse because our familiar routines are disrupted. However, these times may also be a blessing. They provide us with an invitation to be alone with ourselves and to listen with an open heart. Can we hear God's song in the silence? Can we sense the music of His love that will sustain us even amidst our suffering? Can we be instruments of God's healing as our crises unfold?

CHAPTER SIXTEEN

JESUS AND JUDAS

"Father, forgive them; they do not know what they are doing."
—Jesus of Nazareth

We Catholics believe in the forgiveness of sins. God's mercy is infinitely greater than our failings.

Jesus loved Judas to the end—and beyond. He saw the goodness in Judas' heart and chose him to be one of his inner circle of disciples. They travelled the countryside together, conversing intimately. They ate and slept in each others' company. Their home was the outdoors, in the sunlight and under the stars. Even though Jesus was his teacher, they became close friends.

Judas had the privilege of walking in the footsteps of the Master. He felt Jesus' personal love of him and saw his care for the crowds. He witnessed the miracles and the authority with which Jesus spoke. Jesus taught the crowds in parables, but explained his secrets to those closest to him. Judas experienced the extraordinary power of Jesus' personality, words, and actions. He also shared Jesus' most intimate moments at meals with friends and at his last supper.

What went wrong in Judas' relationship with his master, teacher, and friend? What possessed him to betray the one who loved him so much? When did the darkness first enter his heart? When did the idea occur to him that he could make money handing over his beloved?

Jesus knew Judas intimately. He sensed the turning of his heart and the treachery. They shared his last meal as a devoted family. They broke bread and drank wine together. During the meal, Jesus knew what Judas was thinking and did not try to stop him. Even though he had extraordinary power and influence, he did not impose his will on his friend. With great sadness, he respected his freedom.

While praying in the garden, Judas approached Jesus accompanied by an armed band intent on violence. He greeted Jesus with a kiss, and Jesus embraced him as a friend. With a heavy heart, he told him to do what he had to do. Jesus surrendered to the treachery of his friend without resistance. He never hated his beloved friend, even while being handed over for a cruel and shameful death.

At some point, Judas awakened to the wickedness of his deed. Regret overcame him. He tried to return the money paid for innocent blood, but the temple leaders refused to accept it. Remorseful and despondent, Judas hanged himself. In that desperate moment, he forgot Jesus' message of forgiveness. He believed that his sin was greater than God's mercy.

We may relive this story of love and disappointment in our relationships. Jesus was the ideal master, teacher, and friend, who lived with a perfectly wise and loving heart, yet still suffered the rejection of someone closest to him. Out of love he respected the freedom of his beloved, even if he knew they were choosing a path of destruction. He never considered pressuring anyone into doing what was right.

As parents, do we blame ourselves when our children choose a path different from the one we envisioned for them, or when they become estranged from us? "Where did I go wrong? I taught them better than that!" we lament.

As spouses, while loving wholeheartedly, do we get down on ourselves when our partners become withdrawn, moody, or rejecting? "Is he or she mad at me?" we worry.

As teachers, do we accuse ourselves of incompetence when our students refuse to learn? "Why can't I get through to them?" we ask.

As psychologists, do we feel inadequate when our patients do not improve or even commit suicide? "What could I have done differently?" we wonder.

Our best efforts at loving are always mixed with humility and hope. We can only plant seeds, as Jesus did, but cannot completely manage the flowering. A traditional saying reminds us, "No seed ever sees the fruit." Yet we can have hope in the everlasting power of love, which can later bear fruit in unexpected ways. Faithful love waters those seeds.

We may believe that Judas deserves to be condemned forever to the lowest regions of hell because of his unforgivable sin. However, there is a legend that Judas was finally redeemed in India in the last century. After numerous incarnations, he was liberated from the ongoing cycle of birth and rebirth. Jesus' love for him never died and brought new life. The power of Jesus' love working through us can also bring similar surprising outcomes.

CHAPTER SEVENTEEN

OUR PERSONAL DIGNITY

"Then God said, 'Let us make man in
our image, after our likeness.'"
—Genesis 26: 1

We Catholics believe the Scriptures are God's Word of love to us. He reveals that we are His beloved, made in His image and likeness.

Our nation is founded on the belief in the dignity of the human person. Our Declaration of Independence states: "We hold these truths to be self-evident, that all men are created equal, that they are endowed by their Creator with certain inalienable rights, that among these are Life, Liberty and the pursuit of Happiness." The first ten amendments to our Constitution was the enumeration of a Bill of Rights that guarantees the protection of basic human rights for all citizens.

The conviction of personal dignity arose from the rational approach of the Enlightenment that our founding ancestors espoused. It is also rooted in biblical faith. The Genesis creation story proclaims: "Then God said, 'Let us make man in our image, after our likeness....God created man in his image; in the image of God he created him; male and female he created them. God blessed them saying: 'Be fertile and multiply; fill the earth and subdue it. Have dominion over the fish of the sea, the birds of the air, and all the living things that move on the earth.'" (Genesis 1: 26-29) In our conviction of the dignity of the human person, faith and reason join hands.

Unfortunately, our history has betrayed this fundamental ideal. We became confused about our definition of humanity, excluding and persecuting many. Arriving in the new world, we treated the Native Americans as less than human and displaced them from their land in the name of manifest destiny. We brought slaves from Africa to serve us and discriminated against people of color throughout our history. Protestants mistrusted and persecuted the papist Catholics. Women, considered inferior, were deprived of the right to vote until a century ago. And today our prejudices have metastasized to consume those of differing sexual orientation, ethnic background, and social status. We have not become the envisioned melting pot in which we blend together in our diversity. Instead, we are a broken mosaic of clashing colors.

POLITICS TURNS PERSONAL

In recent years, the lack of personal respect infects politics. Americans look upon each other as friends or foes according to differing political persuasions. Instead of rational discourse, political debates often degenerate into personal attacks and name-calling. Candidates are addressed as crooked Hilary, sleepy Joe, and Trump the narcissist. The motivation of candidates is questioned. They are judged as dishonest, corrupt, self-serving, and power-hungry. They are accused of attempts to steal our freedom, wealth, or power. In the wake of this personal mistrust, political conversations become acrimonious. Open discussion of diverse views ceases. Because of the fear of personal retribution, politicians vote along party lines and ignore their own consciences and judgment. Compromises are never reached, and stalemates rule Washington.

What happens in Washington radiates throughout society. Families and friendships are polarized and broken over political differences of opinion. One patient complained, "The family holiday gatherings are tense. We have to avoid any political discussions, or an argument will break out. My liberal son refuses to attend if his conservative uncle comes." Another patient lamented, "I've lost many friends in the past few years over politics. I just can't stand being around the Trump supporters with all their conspiracy theories." A third patient confessed, "If anyone rejects my firmly held ideas, they reject me." They closely identify with their thinking. "I am my thoughts," they seem to tell themselves. Being on the right side of political issues, then, becomes more important than maintaining long-standing relationships.

Social media feeds the personalized and polarized thinking. The more time we spend surfing the Internet, the more our opinions are galvanized, confirming our biases. The social media algorithms are set up to cater to our preferences. We are constantly fed products and stories that reinforce our desires and points of view. The goal is to sell us more. We receive slanted news and anecdotes. We connect with like-minded fellow surfers that further harden our views and cause us to mistrust other opinions. In the process, we lose trust in the mainline media which intends to address the general public. We also mistrust government institutions. Confident of our Google education, we say, "I just don't buy the conventional narrative."

The personal attacks and polarized thinking undermine democracy and civil discourse.

PARANOID MINDSET

Many factors, of course, contribute to the polarized thinking, the "we-they" mentality, including a paranoid mindset. As a psychologist in private practice, I have been observing a growing trend in my patients toward suspicious, negative thinking. They feel vulnerable and powerless. They lament, "Our society is falling apart. It's worse now than it has ever been." They see the universe and its hidden agents as being against them. Living in a constant state of emergency, they feel exhausted. "Fate is not on my side," they complain. They feel disaffected and wronged by life, which is not unfolding as they wish it would, and look for someone to blame. Without acknowledging it, they fall into a helpless victim role.

Our materialistic, consumerist culture fosters a paranoid outlook on life. We are encouraged to want more and more. The promise is that the more we have, the happier we will be. Our cravings increase, and we tend to identify who we are with what we have. That only breeds insecurity. Our escalating desires can never be satisfied. So, we always feel a sense of loss that something is missing. When we do acquire or achieve anything, we fear losing it. We are frightened that someone is waiting to steal what we hold precious: our wealth, power, status, freedom.

In the face of inevitable losses, we do not ask how this happened. Instead, we inquire, "Who did this to me?" There is always an enemy, often hidden, waiting in the bushes to rob us of our precious possessions. We are ever-alert to signs of a secret threatening presence. Because we identify who we are with what we have, that loss can be catastrophic to our personal well-being.

The paranoid way of thinking grows incrementally. When we lose something we value, for example our wealth or status, we brood and complain about it. We crave even more what we are missing and become angry at being deprived of it. We nurture the idea that we are innocent victims being unjustly persecuted and look for people to blame. They become our enemies. Our anger deepens, and we forget who we are. The anger overwhelms our reasoning capacity. We rationalize our righteousness, determined to seek justice. Violent action, unfortunately, often follows in the wake of these thoughts.

Interestingly, research indicates that 80% of those who voted for President Trump described themselves as angry and aggrieved. They felt like victims of the establishment and found in him a promised rescuer. So identified with the victim role, the question arises, "Who would I be and what would I do when I don't have a bad guy to fight and blame?"

Paranoid thinking makes us miserable, estranged from ourselves and others.

RECOVERING OUR DIGNITY

Is there a way to escape the paranoid mental prison and victim role? Is there a way to recover our dignity as human beings? Definitely, yes! I have a few modest suggestions:

<u>Separate the persons and their ideas:</u>

Paranoid thinking confuses persons with their opinions and behaviors. "You are what you think, say, and do," we imagine. We may tell ourselves, "If you think that way (different from how I think), something must be seriously wrong with you." However, the individual person, with consciousness, is far greater. Our thoughts and reactions are like passing clouds, always changing. We are the stable blue sky. Our thoughts, feelings, and behaviors come from us, but they are not us. They cannot fully express the wonder and mystery of who we are. Jesus commanded us to forgive our enemies. He told us to hate the sin but love the sinner. Often, we are better than our behavior and need to examine ourselves to make our thoughts and actions more in line with the angels of our better nature.

<u>Stop judging and be curious:</u>

We compensate for our sense of helplessness by assuming the role of judge. We pretend we are superior. However, we are more limited than we think. It is a full-time job to know ourselves. We hardly know our own real motivations for what we do. How can we imagine we understand what drives other people? When we assume the role of judge, we use standards which reflect our biases. Our minds are closed. The opposite attitude is to be curious, to have an open mind. The truth is larger than any of us. Each of us has a unique perspective on it. With openness to the unknown, we can learn from each other and enrich our lives.

Focus on what you have, not on what's missing:

The paranoid outlook is preoccupied with what has been or will be taken from us. We are depressed by what we have lost, anxious about what more we can lose, and angry about being wronged. Automatic negative thoughts, called "ANTs," rule our minds. A pessimistic outlook results… and much misery. The antidote to this emotionally painful pessimism is gratitude. We shift attention from what is lacking in our life to what we already have. The mere fact that we are alive is a miraculous blessing. Our world sustains us much more than it deprives us. We receive more from Mother Nature than we could ever give back in return. Our families and community enable us to survive and thrive as human beings.

Awareness of our abundance protects us from the pain of inevitable loss. A poor man is devastated if he loses a dollar. A millionaire barely notices it when he loses a dollar in a transaction. We have been blessed with the precious gifts of life and God's boundless love. "Nothing can separate us from the love of God," St. Paul reminds us. In comparison with such an eternal treasure, the losses of our material goods and wellbeing are of little significance.

Stop blaming and take responsibility:

The more we blame others for our misery, the more we make ourselves dependent on them for our happiness. We make them very powerful. When things go wrong, we tend to ask, "Who did this to me?" Since we cannot change others, we make ourselves helpless in our dependency.

Instead, we can take full responsibility for our own happiness. In reality, we are masters of our own fates. When we face adversity, we can examine how it occurred. We may discover how we played a part in creating our own problems. Then, we may learn to take a more effective approach. We empower ourselves in taking full responsibility for the events of our lives.

Reclaim your own authority:

When we are paranoid, we mistrust others. We live on high alert that somehow others will harm us. Enemies surround us, living in hiding. That is an exhausting way to live. It reveals how insecure we feel about ourselves. In reality, we are much stronger than we think. Others may take away our wealth, status, power, or even physical wellbeing. But no one can touch the core of who we are, our soul which is everlasting. We are God's beloved children. Jesus reminded us that it is not what goes into us that harms us but what comes from our hearts. We are the authors of our lives with the freedom to determine whether or not we live according to our values. The challenge is to learn to trust ourselves, our true nature.

Focus on being, not having:

Our consumerist society invites us to define ourselves externally, by what we have and accomplish. Unfortunately, in the process we become possessed by our possessions. We are enslaved by the lust for more. Instead, our founding ancestors and all the religious traditions invite us to recognize our innate dignity. All of us are born with an infinite value, which cannot be lost, only tarnished by our undignified behavior. If we focus on our true selves, we will be inspired to let our light shine and live according to our highest values.

A lack of personal respect and trust has recently infected our politics. It has polarized our nation and broken relationships. Nevertheless, there is a way out of this gridlock. If we return to our national and spiritual roots and recognize the dignity of every person, the tenor of our political debates will change drastically. We will no longer attack one another. The hostility and violence will end. Then, we can begin sharing ideas to resolve the complex issues facing our great nation. The survival of our democratic society depends on our learning once again how to engage in respectful dialogue.

CHAPTER EIGHTEEN

THE THIRD PANDEMIC

"What does it profit a man if he gains the
whole world and lose his soul?"
—Jesus of Nazareth

We Catholics are people of hope. In our creed we profess our belief in the resurrection of the dead and life everlasting. We are eternal souls, not just bodies, destined to live forever with our Lord.

President Biden marked the anniversary of the January 6th assault on the Capitol with a memorial ceremony. A few dozen congressmen gathered in a hall adjacent to the House chamber where the attack occurred. The President gave a scathing speech in which he decried the threat to democracy and announced, "We are in a battle for the soul of America."

The hall was filled with Democratic representatives and only one Republican, Liz Cheney. The Republicans boycotted the ceremony, claiming it was only a political ploy. Democrats labeled the January 6th event in which hundreds of demonstrators entered the Capitol to disrupt the certification of the 2020 election as an "insurrection." Many Republicans called it a protest against a stolen election. Both sides claimed they were being patriotic, defending the Constitution. Each side appeared to live in an alternate reality in their interpretation of the event.

In his speech, President Biden accused former President Trump of instigating the insurrection. He said, "The former President of the United States of America created and spread a web of lies about the 2020 election." Trump countered by charging the Democrats with "lies and polarizations." The division and bitterness within our country and our own hearts was dramatically displayed to the world by the January 6th event and its memorial.

President Biden highlighted an overlooked element in the current pandemic. He said we are in a "battle for the soul of America." What is at stake in the battle? How is our soul being threatened? How can we recover it?

A THIRD PANDEMIC: SOUL-SICKNESS

Another pandemic is unfolding in the bitter fighting and polarization over how to address the COVID-19 public health crisis. The contentiousness is affecting our physical health, our mental-emotional wellbeing, and even our spiritual vigor. Our struggles through the pandemic impact our bodies, minds, and souls—the whole person and the entire nation. The disease is contagious, infecting us at ever-deeper levels.

The pandemic began two and a half years ago with the global infection of the Coronavirus, threatening our physical health. Millions have been infected, become seriously ill, and died around the world. Scientists from all nations worked tirelessly to develop a safe and effective vaccine. New treatments are being developed. Governments initiate policies, such as mask and vaccine mandates and social restrictions, to curb the spread of COVID-19. While many question the strategies, there is evidence that we are making significant gains on the medical front.

A second pandemic regarding our psychological wellbeing is currently taking hold. Many of us suffer from pandemic fatigue. We are emotionally drained by the disruptions in our lives fighting the virus. We are depressed. We grieve the losses of our loved ones, of our financial security, of our familiar routines. Our children especially miss out on social and educational opportunities that inhibit their development. We are also anxious. Uncertainty about the future and the possibility of more deadly viruses grips us. And we are angry. We believe we should not have had to suffer so much. The increased rates of clinical depression and anxiety, suicide, substance abuse, and violence document the depth and breadth of the mental health crisis. More are dying psychologically than have died medically from COVID-19.

President Biden alerted us to the third pandemic, the current threat to the well-being of our soul. He claimed that our identity as an American people is at stake: who we are, have been, and should ever be. He pointed to the core values of our Founding Fathers that define us as Americans. He said, "Deep in the heart of America burns a flame lit almost 250 years ago—of liberty, freedom and equality." He added, "We're a nation of laws; of order, not chaos; of peace, not violence." These values are being ignored, at the peril of our soul.

As Biden suggests, the core of who we are, our character, is defined by our values. We all have a conscience by which we perceive and choose our life-guiding values. However, today, we live in a social and political climate in which there is confusion about what is true and false, what is right and wrong. With so much disinformation and deceit, we do not know who or what to believe. Was the election stolen? Is the pandemic a hoax? Are vaccines really safe and effective? Are masks and lockdowns necessary? Do we need vaccine mandates? We do not know whom to trust. We lack reliable authorities and are not sure we can even trust ourselves. So, we feel lost.

In short, we suffer from an existential anxiety that touches our souls. A deep, dark doubt clouds our thinking and confuses our decision-making. We lack a stable moral compass and react to the expediency of the moment. Our self-interested cravings rule. When that doubt takes hold, we feel empty and search for something secure to hang onto.

To avoid the abyss of meaninglessness, we search for an individual, a group, or an ideology that will give us clear and simple answers to the complexity of life. Conservatives may nostalgically long for the "good old days." They place their trust, for example, in political leaders like Donald Trump or in fundamentalist churches. They surrender to them with a blind faith. Liberals may espouse utopian ideologies and causes, for example, regarding social reform and climate change, which they single-mindedly pursue. Our blind trust often leads to fanaticism and intolerance of different opinions. We hide behind a self-righteous indignation. In reality, we are terrified of our hidden doubt being exposed.

We become soul-sick when we believe we possess the whole truth and persecute those who disagree with us. Conversations become hostile arguments. Disagreements become personal. Often, we demean and belittle those of differing opinions as naïve, ignorant, or deceitful, as if we know their hidden motivations. Sadly, disagreements about how to address the complex issues of the pandemic tear apart families, friendships, and our nation.

Is there a cure for our soul-sickness?

RESTORING SOUL POWER

Jesus, the physician of souls, asked, "What does it profit a man if he gains the whole world and loses his soul?" (Mark 8:36) Jesus affirmed the supreme importance of caring for our souls, seeking God's kingdom first. We may be proud that we have the right answers and get our way. But if we destroy others, and ourselves, in the process, what have we accomplished? However, returning to universal core values can renew our spirits:

Respect Life:

How precious is every human life! Each possesses undying, immeasurable value, which can never be earned or relinquished. We are made in the image and likeness of God, reflecting His glory. Like God, we are created with the capacity to know and love, which we exercise in freedom.

We are born free. We are free to be ourselves, to think our thoughts, to indulge our tastes, to follow our inclinations, and to behave in any way we decide. God respects our freedom and does not impose His will on us. He invites us to pursue goodness and truth and does not stop us from choosing evil and error. He further allows us to suffer the consequences of whatever we decide.

During the pandemic, many disputes sprang up that often resulted in hostile exchanges. We believed our health and wellbeing depended on the outcome for these debates. For example, there has been great divide over vaccines, whether or not they are needed or should be mandated. Anti-vaxxers are convinced the vaccine is more dangerous than COVID-19 and object to freedom-violating mandates. Those who support vaccines think that those who refuse to be vaccinated are selfish and endanger the public health. These opposing groups can disdain and personally attack one another. Mean-spirited thoughts may arise: "Those who are unvaccinated deserve to get seriously ill." Others may think, "You are naïve and stupid for thinking that way."

What is more harmful? Taking or refusing the vaccine, which affects the health of the body, or the hostile personal attacks that damage the soul, and may have eternal consequences?

In these inevitable pandemic debates, we will survive only if we act out of love instead of hate. Our guiding principle must be the golden rule: treat others the way we want to be treated. We long to be treated with love that is "patient, kind, not jealous, never rude, not self-seeking, not prone to anger nor does it brood over injuries, does not rejoice in what is wrong but rejoices with the truth." (I Cor. 13: 4-6) That becomes the standard for how we treat others.

To remain civil and respectful in any disagreement, we need to separate the person from the opinion. The golden rule teaches that we love the person even if we hate his ideas. Further, our opponent in the debate has the right to hold any view, as do we, even if we consider it erroneous and harmful.

What is most challenging in these controversies is the requirement that we love our opponent in thought, word, and deed. We may be able to restrain ourselves enough to withhold aggressive actions and words. How much more difficult it is to give up hostile thoughts about the person. We are tempted to judge them and their motivations harshly. We may even secretly wish them harm. Jesus warns, "What I say to you is: everyone who grows angry with his brother is liable to judgment....and if he holds him in contempt he risks the fires of Gehenna." (Matthew 6:22) Dire consequences await us when we nurture angry thoughts against another. We create hell on earth.

The seeds of hatred in our minds inevitably flower and spread like weeds. Angry thoughts cannot be suppressed for long and invite retaliation from others. They create a hostile atmosphere in society that sooner or later creates civil unrest and erupts into violence. Over time, the simmering anger leads to wars between nations. All of nature eventually sprouts the violence in earthquakes, droughts, and storms. Our inner world eventually blooms in the outer universe.

Fight for Freedom:

We fight for the truth that will set us free. Conflicts arise because we have different perspectives on what is true and false. In our discussions, we may hate each other's ideas and see each other's positions as untrue and even destructive. In this case, we are called to fight for the truth we believe and explain clearly and respectfully our reasoning. We are obligated to confront the error we see. Deceit and falsehood hold us in bondage. Only living in truth will guarantee our freedom. We cannot be free unless we pursue the truth with open minds and hearts.

Some of the greatest freedom fighters of the last century—Mahatma Gandhi, Martin Luther King, Jr., and Nelson Mandela—offer examples and strategies for maintaining peace in the midst of controversy. All advocated respect for their adversaries while courageously speaking their truth. They decried violence, which would obscure their message. They refused to surrender their freedom to love by engaging in hate.

Martin Luther King, Jr. wrote in his autobiography (*The Autobiography of Martin Luther King, Jr.* Ed. Clayborne Carson. New York: Grand Central Publishing, 1998): "Let us not satisfy our thirst for freedom by drinking from the cup of bitterness and hatred. We must forever conduct our struggle on the high plane of dignity and discipline. We must not allow our creative protest to degenerate into physical violence. Again and again, we must rise to the majestic heights of meeting physical force with soul force." (p. 225) Ill will in our hearts enslaves us. Only soul force can overcome the physical, emotional, and spiritual devastation of the pandemic.

Perform Works of Mercy:

Listening with an open mind and speaking our truth in love will advance the healing of our battered souls. Yet words alone cannot bind our wounds. Actions are required. Compassionate action also opens the minds and hearts of our adversaries, like flowers to sunshine.

Jesus suggested the appropriate actions in his description of the last judgment: "The King will say to those on his right: 'Come. You have my Father's blessing! Inherit the kingdom prepared for you from the creation of the world. For I was hungry, and you gave me food. I was thirsty, and you gave me drink. I was a stranger, and you welcomed me, naked, and you clothed me. I was ill, and you comforted me, in prison, and you came to visit me.'... The just will ask him: 'Lord, when did we see you hungry or thirsty or away from home or naked or ill or in prison?'...The king will answer them: 'I assure you, as often as you did it for one of my least brothers, you did it for me.'" (Matthew 25: 34-40) During the pandemic and even now, there is an urgent need to show mercy to those suffering material hardships. What we do for others, we do for Christ. How we care for the physical needs of others has an everlasting consequence. We experience a taste of heaven.

The whole person cries out to be cared for. Consequently, we are concerned for the physical, mental, and spiritual wellbeing of others. The traditional spiritual works of mercy complement the above corporal works: to instruct the ignorant; to counsel the doubtful; to admonish the sinner; to bear wrongs patiently; to forgive offenses willingly; to comfort the afflicted; to pray for the living and the dead. In this third pandemic, there is an even greater urgency to care for each other's spiritual needs.

Small acts of kindness can make a significant difference. Mother Teresa famously said, "Not all of us can do great things. But we can do small things with great love." The seeds of love in our thoughts, words, and deeds also flower, creating a garden of peace and harmony. They invite those around us to respond in a loving manner. The love, openness, and acceptance create an atmosphere in society where all will be inclined to engage in fruitful dialogue. Violence between nations and wars may eventually end. Nature will reflect the tranquility that resides in our hearts.

As the pandemic unfolds, we realize its devastating impact on our bodies, minds, and spirits. The disease is highly contagious, infecting us at ever deeper levels. Now it is clear that the growing mistrust, deceit, and hostility have made us soul-sick as individuals and a nation. We feel lost. Some despair of recovery. Nevertheless, we Americans are a resilient, resourceful people. Within the suffering of this illness, we have the medicine for our recovery. Our nation was founded on high ideals. By returning to our core values—forsaking hatred for love, judgment for compassion, deceit for honesty—we can rise above the ashes of our anguish.

CHAPTER NINETEEN

THE FULL LIFE

"I came that they might have life and have it to the full."
—Jesus of Nazareth

We Catholics pray for the coming of God's Kingdom, a kingdom of peace and forgiveness.

The recent school shootings have shocked our nation and the world. Innocent children at Robb Elementary School in Uvalde, Texas, at Oxford High School outside Detroit, and at other schools around the country have been gunned down. In every case, the lone shoot came armed in battle gear, ready to kill and be killed. He was a soldier on a mission known only to him. We outsiders see his action as a senseless killing of the innocent. In stunned amazement, we ask, "Why?" We cannot imagine his reasoning for the killing spree. "He could only be mentally ill," we tell ourselves.

Commentators report an increasing number of mass shootings in our country. They call America "the most violent country on the planet, who loves guns." How can we stop the violence? Politicians enter the fray, predictably taking partisan positions. The Democrats say we have a gun problem and look for ways of limiting access to weapons. The Republicans claim we have a people problem and must address mental illness in our society. Both, of course, are right. But will they be willing to work together to effectively address the issue?

We must look deeper for any lasting solution. I believe that violence in our society is a human problem. It reveals the heart of darkness that possesses all of us to some extent. Hopefully, these horrific events will lead each of us to a searching personal examination.

ANATOMY OF VIOLENCE

We imagine that the real problem is violence. If we just control access to the instruments of violence, guns, the impact of the violent behavior will be lessened, though not eliminated. However, a deeper look at the psychology of violent behavior reveals that it is a symptom, more than the root problem. It arises from anger. We nurture feelings of anger because they serve a purpose for us. Anger gives us the illusion of power when we feel powerless inside. Attacking others, then, makes us feel in control of our lives. Having the power of life and death over others can be intoxicating, especially when we feel empty inside.

Anger, then, reveals a deeper sense of loss. It is frustrated desire. We want something we are not getting. Or we are getting something we do not want. We believe that something important is missing in our lives. Often, we ask, "Who did this to me?" We blame others for depriving or harming us and attack them for persecuting us. They cause our misery. We feel like victims who have been wronged. We may even feel justified in our aggression because we see ourselves as innocent and righteous. Our revenge feels sweet.

Beneath this sense of loss is some desire not being met. The word desire comes from the root word meaning "from the stars." We are striving for more, entertaining some ambition. Of course, if we aim for the stars, we will always feel disappointed and deprived. When we lose what we hold dear, we feel sadness, which can progress to a depressed mood. When we fear losing what we value highly, we feel anxious. In short, depression involves past losses, while anxiety concerns possible future losses.

Violent behavior occurs as the end, not the beginning, of a chain reaction. Unrealized expectations lead to feelings of loss and frustration. We may then become depressed or anxious as a result. These moods generate angry feelings which we direct either against ourselves or others. Suicide or shootings may result.

Researchers tell us that nearly a third of Americans suffer from clinical levels of anxiety and depression. That should not be surprising. We are an ambitious culture, entertaining high expectations about the good life. In the extreme, some of us "want it all, and want it now." The "it" is physical comfort, pleasure and possessions. With such thinking, we set ourselves up for living with a profound sense of loss and disappointment. We can never get enough. That is fertile ground for the seeds of anger and violent behavior.

Violence driven by frustrated desire is not new. It happened between Cain and Abel, the sons of Adam and Eve. Tragically, the slaughter of innocent children is also not a new phenomenon. It occurs regularly in wars. We have documentation of it 2000 years ago in the New Testament. Herod massacred the boys younger than two years old in Bethlehem in an attempt to eliminate Jesus. He believed that Jesus was the coming King of the Jews who would threaten his power. His murderous act, as reprehensible as it was, was driven by a blind ambition. He wanted to keep his throne—at any cost. He was willing to kill to protect his self-interest.

The violence within society and our own hearts is driven by some ambition, whether conscious or not. What are we willing to die for—or kill for? What do we value more than even life itself? Parents tell me they are willing die for and kill to protect their children. Patriots willingly kill and sacrifice their lives for freedom. Socrates gave up his life, drinking the hemlock, out of loyalty to the State. Jesus surrendered his life on the cross to testify to the truth he taught and to give us new life. What ambition drives us? How noble, how large, is that value for which we dedicate our lives?

TRUE RICHES

In the Sermon on the Mount (Matthew 5: 1--7: 29), Jesus speaks to the angry about the way to peace. Our uncontrolled anger destroys relationships, robs us of inner peace, and diminishes our spirit. Jesus invites us to delve deeply into our hearts of darkness to discover God's plentiful mercy.

He begins by instructing us that controlling our violent behavior is not enough. We must address the roots of anger in our inner dispositions. Angry thoughts and words eventually erupt into murderous behavior. Jesus said, "You have heard the commandment imposed on your forefathers, 'You shall not commit murder; every murderer shall be liable to judgment.' What I say to you is: everyone who grows angry with his brother shall be liable to judgment; any man who uses abusive language toward his brother shall be answerable to the Sanhedrin, and if he holds him in contempt, he risks the fires of Gehenna."

After inviting us to look inward, Jesus teaches that the desires in our hearts can lead to either misery or joy, to a sense of emptiness or fullness. He said, "Do not lay up for yourselves an earthly treasure. Moths and rust corrode; thieves break in and steal. Make it your practice instead to store up heavenly treasure, which neither moths nor rust corrode nor thieves break in and steal. Remember, where your treasure is, there your hear is also.....No man can serve two masters. He will either hate one and love the other or be attentive to one and despise the other. You cannot give yourself to God and money."

Jesus presents a stark choice. We make either the pursuit of our earthly treasures or heavenly treasures our ultimate concerns. Of course, we must attend to our earthly treasures, our physical needs, to survive. However, we can become preoccupied with physical comforts, pleasure-seeking, chasing after money, sex, power, and prestige. These can become our ultimate concerns in life, believing that their satisfaction will make us forever happy. Our materialistic, consumer culture preaches this gospel. But Jesus warns that these treasures come and go. If we rely too much on them for our happiness, we will inevitably be disappointed. We will be terrified of losing them and fight to the death those who threaten to take them away.

What are the heavenly treasures? Jesus invites us to look around and see for ourselves. He said, "Look at the birds in the sky....Learn a lesson from the way the flowers grow." Nature can teach us if we just pay attention. Jesus observes that the animals and plants do not toil or worry, yet they flourish because of God's care. "Are not you more important than they?" Jesus asks. Through nature, God provides us with what we need, even more than enough.

God has already showered His gifts upon us. Jesus said, "Your heavenly Father knows all that you need. Seek first his kingship over you, his way of holiness, and all these things will be given you besides." Gratitude for the abundance we already have extinguishes the flame of anger.

Finally, Jesus teaches us God's way of holiness. It is the way of forgiveness. He said, "You have heard the commandment, 'You shall love your countryman but hate your enemy.' My command to you is: love your enemies, pray for your persecutors. This will prove that you are sons of your heavenly Father, for his sun rises on the bad and the good, he rains on the just and the unjust." Jesus proclaimed that only forgiveness, loving our enemies, can release us from the grip of anger.

In facing our rising anger, Jesus invites us to ask ourselves these questions:

- What are you so angry about?
- What does your anger accomplish?
- What do you treasure most?
- Is your heart large enough to seek heavenly treasure?
- Do you believe in the abundance of God's grace, or do you live with a sense of emptiness?
- How willing are you to forgive yourself and others?

HEALING ANGER'S WOUND

When I meet with angry patients, I ask them, "What are you really angry about?" Not surprisingly, they have difficulty expressing precisely the cause of their anger. They may take their anger out on themselves and others but are unclear about its real source. Together, we unpeel the onion, the layers of hurt, fear, and unfulfilled desires hidden beneath the angry façade. We acknowledge that their anger is like a poison that only harms them.

Then, we explore their unmet needs. We look at what they are able to do to for themselves. Through this examination, they begin to discern what they can control and what they cannot. They learn where they need to take courageous action and when to accept a limitation. Like a good card player, they recognize when they need to hold and when to fold. As they gain a sense of power over their lives, their helplessness and impotent rage diminish.

As my patients progress through therapy, they begin to take more responsibility for their lives. They are less angry and do not blame others for their problems. They ask themselves, "What really matters to me?" Their perspective gradually shifts. They focus less on what is missing in their lives and attend to what they have. "How can I develop my gifts and get what I really want?' they ask. Gratitude replaces sadness and anxiety. They rejoice in the fullness of their lives, not bemoaning the emptiness. Their freely chosen values guide them and bring them joy. Most discover within themselves a desire to serve others.

Violence will end in our society when we are all at peace with ourselves. As Mahatma Gandhi, the great peacemaker, said, "You must be the change you wish to see in the world." We may take important intermediate steps, such as gun control, better identification of at-risk individuals, and improved mental health care. But in the end, each of us must do the work of addressing the anger, fear, and sadness in our own hearts that make us prone to many forms of violence in our relationships.

CHAPTER TWENTY

PEACEMAKING

"For the sake of those ten, I will not destroy it."
—Genesis 18: 32

We Catholics believe in the promises of the beatitudes: "Blest too the peacemakers; they shall be called children of God."

A long-awaited family trip to Portugal yielded several surprises. Not only the natural beauty of the country but especially the innate friendliness of the people enchanted me. I was travelling with my five-year-old grandson and his parents. My grandson became a magnet for loving attention from strangers on the street. Older women blew him kisses. Children wanted to dance with him to the rhythm of the frequent street musicians we encountered. We felt embraced by the Portuguese people even though we were foreigners ignorant of their language and culture.

We also met several Americans who had recently moved to Portugal. They were drawn by the beauty, peace, and unhurried pace of the place. They said, "We feel safe here. Everyone is so friendly and makes us feel welcome." We enquired further about their dramatic decision to relocate. They explained, "We don't feel safe in America. There's so much violence. We want to protect our kids and have them grow up in a place of peace. We don't want to deal with all the negativity back home."

I feel the same distress about our nation's drift toward violence, political infighting, and paranoia. While some want to get away from the chaos, others choose to jump into the fray. They take sides in the political debate and argue their positions vehemently. Their anger and blood pressure rise as they argue with their family, friends, neighbors, and even strangers. They say, "Unless we stand up for the truth, evil will win out!" Over time, however, they appear to be swept away by waves of angry self-righteousness. They begin to be indistinguishable from their opponents whose narrow-mindedness, irrationality, and hostility they detest.

The heightened conflicts and violence in our society can certainly be demoralizing. For some of us who hate confrontation, we choose to withdraw. We want to find some safe place for ourselves. For others of us who enjoy the fight, we engage in arguing and protesting. We hope for others to convert to our point of view.

Personally, I am not discouraged by all the conflicts in our society. Conflict is inevitable and necessary for growth. It is a sign of life. In a society as diverse as ours, people will have a wide variety of opinions on any given topic—gun control, abortion, climate change, immigration, racial and economic equality, pandemic strategies, and so forth. Our democracy thrives on the exchange of differing ideas and open debate. Even though we appear to have reached stalemates on so many issues, which heighten our frustration, I believe that we are in the midst of some hidden process from which new life will emerge.

People may call me a naïve optimist, and they may be right. However, I see myself as a hopeful realist. I love my country and its position of responsibility in the world. I try to keep the big picture in mind. From a global perspective, this moment of intense conflict may be the birth pains of a better world facing unprecedented problems. Perhaps we are only hearing discordant notes in the great symphony of life. Therefore, I choose not to withdraw in helpless confusion and resignation or drown in hostile confrontations. For me, this is a time to roll up my sleeves for some hard work and welcome the controversy.

In the midst of these warring factions, how can we maintain a stance of peace? How can we be peacemakers? Grace is everywhere. What is the grace of the moment?

PRAYER OF ST. FRANCIS

St. Francis of Assisi lived in a time of turmoil. He was seized by the grace of the moment and renewed a decaying Church. A popular prayer inspired by him can offer guidance in our troubled times. Let me quote that prayer:

"Lord, make me an instrument of your peace.

Where there is hatred, let me bring love.

Where there is offense, let me bring pardon.

Where there is discord, let me bring union.

Where there is error, let me bring truth.

Where there is despair, let me bring hope.

Where there is darkness, let me bring your light.

Where there is sadness, let me bring joy.

O Master, let me not seek as much to be consoled as to console,

to be understood as to understand,

to be loved as to love,

for it is in giving that one receives,

it is in self-forgetting that one finds,

it is in pardoning that one is pardoned,

it is in dying that one is raised to eternal life.

The prayer begins with a request: "Make me an instrument of your peace." We approach God, our Higher Power, however, we conceive Him, asking to be peacemakers. We seek to be God's instrument, not our own, in bringing His peace to the world. We make this prayer because we are aware of our own limitations. Our efforts at peace have failed. The solutions to our problems elude us. As Albert Einstein famously stated, "No problem is ever solved in the same consciousness that was used to create it." So, we ask for a higher consciousness, a wise mind, in approaching our disturbing situation.

Next, the prayer expresses accurately what we are experiencing today. Our society and our hearts are filled with discord, error, despair, darkness, and sadness. The antidote is to do the opposite. So, we aspire to bring union, truth, hope, light, and joy to our broken world. We know that peace will come only if we personally commit to the higher road of our wise minds. Deep in our hearts we also know that only love will conquer hatred and bring lasting peace.

The prayer then recommends specific actions to fulfill our aspirations. These counsels direct us to act against our natural instinct to focus exclusively on our own pain and care only for ourselves. All of us are suffering together in this hostile environment. No one is exempt from the pain and confusion. We cling stubbornly to our ideas as a way of protecting ourselves from insecurity. Our obstinacy masks our misery. Instead of looking to others for comfort, we need to recognize the suffering of those around us and seek to console them. Others need to know we empathize with their pain.

A wall of misunderstanding separates us. We have become trapped in our own mental prisons of cherished opinions. Instead of feeling aggrieved that no one understands us, we are called to make the effort first to understand others' perspectives. We need especially to dialogue with those with whom we disagree most. In all these controversies, there is no absolute right or wrong. We are all right and hold some grain of a larger truth.

In all of our hostile encounters, we feel unloved. Families and friendships are torn apart by differences of political views. If people reject our cherished views, we feel personally attacked. "Love me, love my ideas," we mistakenly think. We make the error that we are what we think. Instead of waiting for others to approach us in love or apologize, we pray to take the first step of love in seeking reconciliation. We love without expecting a return.

The prayer ends with the ultimate reasons for our peacemaking efforts. It is based on a belief that reverses the assumptions of our culture. Our American culture proclaims, "Look out for number one!" We are ruled by the law of competition which states, "The winner takes all." Only the fittest survive. The prayer reverses these cultural assumptions with the higher law of self-giving. It is in giving, in forgetting ourselves, in pardoning, and in dying to ourselves that we achieve the fullness of life we seek.

IMPACT OF THE FEW

The magnitude of the task may discourage us from working for peace. So many Americans are at war with each other over so many political issues. How can the stalemate and hostility be overcome? In the spirit of democracy, we Americans believe in the power of numbers. Our nation appears almost equally divided in the standoff, neither side willing to budge. Neither side can achieve a clear majority to resolve the conflicts.

We ask ourselves, "How can my puny efforts make a difference? I only have the power of one vote."

St. Francis and his prayer exemplify the power of the few in the face of the many. His life changed the course of history. Many men and women have had such an influence. The 20th century has been shaped by individuals such as Mahatma Gandhi, Mother Teresa, Dorothy Day, Martin Luther King, Nelson Mandela, and many more. We may think of them as great persons, while we think of ourselves as small and insignificant.

However, our spiritual traditions, which reflect our higher consciousness, remind us of the power of the few. For example, when God threatened to destroy Sodom and Gomorrah because of their evil ways of life, Abraham bargained with God to spare the city (Genesis 18: 20-32). He pleaded that if only 50 innocent people could be found there, would God agree to withhold his judgment? Abraham negotiated God down to spare the city for only ten innocent people. God responded, "For the sake of those ten, I will not destroy it."

There is a Jewish legend that the stability of the world is supported by 36 unknown men and women of virtue at any given moment. If that number decreases, our world will fall apart. The number 36 is a symbolic number for 6 times 6 which represents all of creation. Those 36 live two lives whole-heartedly: both for themselves and for others, loving both God the Father and Mother. That group of 36 is never constant. At any given moment, anyone, including you and me, can be fully awake and a blessing to someone, maintaining the balance of our world.

In the Christian tradition, of course, the sacrificial life and death of Jesus of Nazareth, redeemed the whole world. Jesus called his disciples to follow in his footsteps, reminding them that no one's life lacks divine significance.

We become peacemakers by first healing our own divided hearts. The divisions in society reflect our own inner conflicts. The hatred in our hearts keeps us from inner tranquility and social peace. Mahatma Gandhi, the great peacemaker, taught, "You must be the change you wish to see in the world." To live the prayer of St. Francis, we must first beg God to make us instruments of His peace. Serenity must reign within us. The small seeds of our peace-filled lives will then bear fruit in a surprising abundance.

CHAPTER TWENTY ONE

CATCHING COVID

"I have been crucified with Christ..."
—Paul of Tarsus

We Catholics believe in the power of the passion, death, and resurrection of Jesus the Christ.

The new strains of COVID-19 were so contagious I believed eventually we would all become infected. I was not worried, though. After all, I had been double vaccinated and boosted. The new strains were less deadly, and I believed I was well protected. I trust science.

Yet, I was still stunned when I tested positive for COVID. I had slight congestion for a few days which was less annoying than a common cold. I had no fever, headache, body aches, or fatigue—typical signs of COVID. However, when our office secretary tested positive for COVID, I decided to take a home test. Much to my surprise, I tested positive. I didn't want to believe it. So, I took a second test. The same result.

Waves of worry swept over me. I am one of those vulnerable elderly even though I rationalized my immunity from serious illness. I know COVID has killed millions around the world. I began imagining the worst. How long would I be out of commission? Could these mild symptoms become serious? Could I become one of those COVID long-haulers with continuous and recurring symptoms? So much is unknown about this virus that it leaves room for nightmarish fantasies.

Upon learning my diagnosis, I immediately called my family and some friends to inform them. I reassured them that I felt fine, except for a little congestion. I was probably trying to reassure myself more than them. Next, I went to my office after hours and called all the patients I had met for the past few days to inform them of my test results. I also contacted friends I had seen. My anxious mind entertained the horror of infecting many others and causing serious illness. I felt guilty for waiting four days to test myself after the first symptoms appeared. "It wasn't even as bad as a cold and couldn't possibly be COVID!" I had told myself.

FLAT TIRE DREAM

That night I recorded a dream that revealed to me my reaction to this startling news. I have been writing a dream journal for many years and have found it helpful to keep in touch with my deeper, more hidden, less conscious reactions. The following is my dream:

"I leave my car at the side of the road. I have to change three tires. Then, I go to work in a factory, bringing the tires with me. After work, my coworkers drive me in the wrong direction. I tell them to turn around to go to my car. They talk about needing money for gas. I pull out a dollar bill from my wallet and offer it. I wonder how I will change the tires. I ask myself if I will need to call a tow truck."

Dreams seem to be bizarre nonsense. They are if we try to interpret them literally. In fact, dreams speak in images and metaphorical language that point the way to deeper subconscious meanings. If we look at them as metaphors revealing what we ignore in our conscious life, we can gain a glimpse of our unconscious mind at work. Dreams reveal aspects of our personality interacting with our world. The symbolic language and events of dreams can elucidate our inner reactions to current life events.

I entitled this dream "Tire Change" and view it as my deeper reaction to the news of my positive COVID test. Having COVID-19 for me is like having a flat tire that sidelines me from my activities. Since only three tires are flat, I am not completely disabled. I rely on my coworkers, who are family and friends, to help me get back to my car, so I can regain control of my life. They are willing to help, but still I must direct them to my car and recovery. I feel indebted to them and want to pay them back in some way. I am in a quandary about how I will change the tires and get back on the road of my usual life. How much help will I need? My inability to drive my car with the flat tires suggests my feelings of being out of control with this illness.

Now I am fully recovered. Looking back, the healing has been not only of my body, but also of my mind and emotions. I grappled with making sense of the illness. These are some of the reflections I had at the time.

THE PASSION

Joseph Campbell, the renowned expert on myths, famously stated, "The cave you fear to enter holds the treasure you seek." My fear of COVID is palpable. The pandemic is not a hoax. I try to run away from my anxiety, to rationalize it, but I cannot avoid it. Having COVID gives me an opportunity to explore the deep meaning of my fear of being sick to discover its treasure.

To find that deeper meaning, I am drawn to the wisdom of my faith. St. Paul wrote, "I have been crucified with Christ, and the life I now live is not my own; Christ is living in me." (Galatians 20: 20) I see this illness as a sharing in the passion of Christ, which is the way to new life. Jesus constantly reminded his disciples that they must lose their small selves in order to gain a fuller life. My reflections take me in several directions:

First of all, being sick with COVID-19 joins me with the billions around the world who are struggling through this two-and-a-half-year pandemic. We are all suffering together. No one is alone. In fact, Christ suffers with, in, and through us all. I am fortunate that my case is mild. I am not undergoing the devastating physical, emotional, and economic effects of this dreadful disease that others have. However, I have a glimpse into their experience which creates a bond with them.

Second, my fear of being sick exposes my small, clinging self. It shows what I grasp onto desperately and am afraid to lose. Of course, I cling to the health of my body. If my physical health disappears, who would I be and what would I do? The illness isolates me and invites me to confront my fear of being alone. I cannot control the course of this illness. My obsession with being in control of my life is challenged. I am attached to my work and routines which are interrupted against my will. The list can go on with further reflection.

Third, COVID suddenly disrupts our lives and isolates us. At the root of my fear of being sick is my terror of dying. I prefer to deny the reality of my inevitable death and not think about it. Death will mean the loss of everyone and everything I hold dear, including my life in the body. That frightens me now. It is also humiliating that I have so little control over my life and cannot be the master of the universe as I secretly fantasize. Perhaps this illness is an opportunity to prepare me for my eventual death, as I slowly learn to let go of my obsessive attachments.

Next, when I learned about my positive test, I did my own personal contact tracing. I felt responsible for spreading this potentially deadly disease, even if unknowingly. It appears that I became infected at a social gathering with a group of friends. We spent a night on the town and mixed with crowds at two bars. At least two others from our group have been infected. I feel a bond of compassion with them. We have reached out to each other to offer support and encouragement. Suffering illness can embitter us, if resented. Or it can open our hearts to be more compassionate.

Fourth, being sick and staying home can teach me patience. In our society, patience is in short supply. We want it all, and we want it now. Illness stops us dead in our tracks. We are forced to be alone and quiet with ourselves, giving us an opportunity to listen to the still voice in our hearts. What can we learn about ourselves in the solitude? For recovery, we also need to get out of our heads and listen to our bodies. What does the wisdom of our bodies tell us we need in the moment?

Finally, I have been touched by how many family and friends have reached out to me. My illness has inspired their compassion, concern, and generosity. Their loving embrace heals me more than I can say. I am filled with gratitude for them. This illness has brought us all closer together. When Christ was lifted up on the cross, he drew the whole world to himself. Sharing his suffering, we are all raised up together.

My hope is that what I experience at an individual level will occur at a global level through this pandemic. Our love, compassion, and generosity can transform this tragedy into a path to new life and closer relationships.

CHAPTER TWENTY TWO

WHAT WE DESERVE

"The unexamined life is not worth living."
—Socrates

We Catholics recognize the importance of regularly examining our consciences, confessing our sins, doing penance, and asking God for forgiveness.

The FBI recently entered former President Trump's private Mar-a-Lago residence with a search warrant. The Department of Justice accused Mr. Trump of illegally confiscating and storing confidential government documents. Predictably, the public and politicians reacted along party lines. On the one hand, many Republicans were outraged at the raid, claiming Trump's innocence. They attacked the Justice Department and FBI for overreaching their roles. On the other hand, many Democrats expressed gleeful satisfaction that Trump would finally pay for his wrongdoing.

Despite these partisan presumptions of innocence and guilt, the reality is that Mr. Trump is neither. He deserves his day in court. In fact, in our judicial system, we consider him innocent until proven guilty. We cannot predict with any assurance the outcome of the investigation. It would be unfair to do so.

The widespread reaction to the event reveals the polarization within our relationships and society. Families, friendships and society are divided over political issues. The polarization further reveals the peculiar way of thinking that has dominated our social conversations. Each side presumes to be right, even before any consideration of the evidence. We make judgments based on our biases and wishes. Our insular thinking believes whatever we want to be true. Believing ourselves infallibly right, we do not listen to opposing views. And we even attack personally those with whom we disagree.

A long-time patient of mine wanted to discuss his reaction to the Mar-a-Lago search, which he considered intrusive and unnecessary. I asked him, "Do you consider Trump an innocent victim or someone who is getting exactly what he deserves." The question halted him in his tracks. "I don't want to say. I have to think about it," he said honestly. I told him this is an important question to consider. "We see others as we are; our judgments of others reflect how we see ourselves," I said. We project our inner world out onto the world around us.

My patient has been in a 40-year marriage marked by constant blaming. He feels like a victim and sees his wife as his persecutor. His wife holds the mirror-opposite opinion. We have been working together to escape the misery-go-round of blame. He persists in trying to understand why his wife is so critical of him. I challenge him, "Why do you spend so much energy trying to understand her? It's a full-time job to know yourself and why you give her so much power over your peace of mind. How can you possibly understand someone else's mind when it is so difficult to know yourself."

What are the roots of this all-or-none thinking? How can we understand this tendency to blame others and feel so helplessly victimized?

PARANOID MINDSET

Beneath this polarized, either-or, thinking can be detected a paranoid mindset. Both sides feel threatened and mistrust each other. We consider our opponents our enemies who entertain some vile motives. "They only want power and will destroy our beloved country" we tell ourselves. We look at our side as innocent victims, and the other side as guilty persecutors.

Melanie Klein, the renowned child psychologist, explains that the roots of this polarized thinking are in childhood. She observes that all infants suffer some degree of birth trauma. They are thrust from the secure warmth of the womb into an unpredictable world. They experience hunger, discomfort, and frustration, depending on the caregiver for relief. Anxiety rules the newborn infant. Klein speculated from her therapy with older children that infants react to the unavoidable frustrations of life out of the womb in two ways.

The first, she calls the "paranoid-schizoid position." In birth, the infant first begins the process of separating from his mother. He primarily uses the defense of splitting, seeing the world as all good or all bad. When he is fed, he experiences the good mother. When he experiences hunger, the mother is bad. The good mother is idealized, loved, and viewed as all-powerful. Those who frustrate his desires are demonized and hated as persecutors. His primitive thinking is black-and-white. No ambiguity or uncertainty can be tolerated.

In the middle of the first year of life, the infant may advance to a more mature reaction called the "depressive position." As the infant's needs are fairly consistently met, he views his mother as both good and bad. He both loves and hates her. However, the infant feels a sense of guilt for hating his mother and desires to repair the damage of his aggression. He grieves his hateful attacks. The infant slowly begins to view himself and others as separate and imperfect. As he matures through the depressive position, he begins to develop a sense of responsibility in owning his anger and making amends. He also learns to tolerate the ambiguity of living in an imperfect world where good and bad are always mixed.

These two ways of infantile thinking persist throughout our lives to some degree.

OUR POLARIZED RELATIONSHIPS

Our relationships and society are so divided because many of us appear to be stuck in the earliest phase of infantile thinking. We are trapped in the "paranoid-schizoid position" without knowing it. The world is split into the all-good and the all-bad.

Viewing events from the paranoid mindset, we look for someone to blame when something goes wrong. "Who did this to me?" we ask. Disagreements become personalized. Discussions seem to become witch-hunts and personal attacks on individuals or groups. We take personal offense over differing opinions, feeling threatened. Some claim, "Those left-wing socialists want to take away our freedom." Others counter, "Those Trump loyalists want to destroy our democracy." In-depth rational conversations about the disputed questions are avoided.

Most issues that affect us all— abortion, climate change, voting rights, and so forth—are complex. However, the paranoid mind sees only in black and white colors. We split the world into good and bad, right and wrong, winners and losers, with nothing in between. We also divide individuals and social groups along the same rigidly defined lines. Those on our side are innocent of any wrongdoing and always right in their views. Those in the out-group we deem guilty of malice and deceit. They are also wrong-headed in their thinking. There is no middle ground. The gap between these opposing positions is so wide that no discussion of alternatives or reconciliation is possible.

We also circle the wagon around the individuals and groups in our camp. We idealize our leaders and demonize our opponents. For example,

Trump can do no wrong in the eyes of his most loyal supporters, while he can do no right according to his detractors. He is a lightning rod for our imbedded ways of thinking. We consider those who criticize him as politically motivated persecutors. His opponents feel victimized by his maneuvering. We overlook the obvious faults of our chosen leaders and exaggerate the weaknesses of our foes. Furthermore, we tend to place our leaders on pedestals and follow them blindly. We find security in our loyalty to our admired individuals and groups.

We feel safe in our blind loyalties but pay a price for it. Unquestioningly following others diminishes our sense of personal responsibility and freedom. Further, the more we blame others for our problems, the more we are dependent on their changing for our solutions. Being a victim may inspire the sympathy of some, but in the process we increase our sense of helplessness. We make those we blame very powerful. Our wellbeing depends more on others than ourselves.

In contrast, when we pursue the more mature path of the depressive position, we begin to reclaim our personal authority. We empower ourselves. When trouble inevitably occurs, we ask, "How did this happen?" Instead of blaming others, we take an objective look at the situation. We assess what factors, including our own missteps, contributed to the problem and what we need to do to find a solution. We may need to admit our own faults and change our behaviors. The approach is objective, impersonal, focused on problem-solving, not people. It frees us to engage with others in exploring alternatives toward a resolution.

How can we escape the misery-go-round of blame that grips our personal relationships and our society? How can we shift from blaming others to taking full responsibility for our lives? How can we develop more mature thinking and reclaim our personal authority?

TAKING FULL RESPONSIBILITY

"We get exactly what we deserve." That statement is not pessimistic. Rather, it is a realistic admission that we are fully responsible for our lives. As adults, we are not innocent, helpless victims. Children may be victims, but not adults. We freely participate in whatever happens to us and invite the consequences. We are both saints and sinners at the same time. When something happens to us we do not like, we can examine if we set ourselves up for it or directly caused it. We are then empowered to make necessary changes to prevent it from happening again. We can change ourselves, but not others.

The 12 steps of Alcoholic Anonymous provide a path for learning to accept full personal responsibility for our lives. The Steps are pragmatic and wise in their guidance. They represent the most original American spirituality of personal transformation, as evidenced by the countless numbers who found recovery through working the steps. For me as a psychologist, the steps summarize well what I am trying to achieve through therapy with my patients. The last three Steps summarize the other nine. They invite us to wake up, clean up, and show up.

Wake Up

When we are caught up in paranoia, we focus outward on our dreaded enemies and their behavior. We judge them according to our standards. In contrast, Step 11 recommends that we shift our focus to ourselves and what our Higher Power demands of us: "Sought through prayer and meditation to improve our conscious contact with God as we understood Him, praying only for knowledge of His will for us and power to carry it out."

To be free and responsible, we first need to wake up to who we really are and what we value most. Whether or not we are religious, that requires spending quiet time alone with ourselves. We may pray, meditate, or just sit. In the solitude, we listen to what arises from our depths. We seek to uncover our true self beneath the façade of our everyday living. Taking the risk of being alone with ourselves, undistracted by our constant busyness, we gain a sense of our infinite depth and worth. In religious terms, we experience ourselves at the core of being made in the image and likeness of God. We share His life.

Our higher self does not float aimlessly. It is anchored in the values we hold dear. In the silence we consider what is most important to us and what we believe really lasts. These ideals give us a sense of stability and direction in our daily living. In religious terms, we seek to know God's will for us in the moment and rely on His grace and power. We are confident that God knows what is best for us. He also wishes to shape us into the likeness of His goodness, love, and truth.

<u>Clean Up</u>

When we see ourselves as victims, we become preoccupied with the faults of our persecutors. We blame them for all our troubles. We also judge them for being so unfair. In contrast, Step Ten suggests we make a regular examination of our own conscience: "Continued to take personal inventory and when we were wrong promptly admitted it."

Next, giving up blaming others requires honesty and humility. We draw strength for our self-examination from the awareness of our own dignity. We look at both our strengths and weaknesses, aware that we are both saint and sinner, innocent and guilty. Aware of our virtues, we seek ways of living them more fully. Aware of our vices, we admit them promptly. We do not try to hide behind a façade of righteousness. Also, we do not beat ourselves up for our wrongdoing. Instead, we recognize we are better than that behavior, make amends to repair the damage, and strive to improve.

We gain a sense of freedom in taking responsibility for all our actions, both good and bad. We do not blame others for the misery our failings invariably cause us. Instead, we empower ourselves by making efforts to correct our faults. We take charge of our lives to avoid future pitfalls from our misguided actions.

Show Up

When we feel so persecuted, we demand that others change so we can feel happy and secure. We place the key of our wellbeing in others' hands. In contrast, Step 12 challenges us to reach out and help others: "Having had a spiritual awakening as the result of these steps, we tried to carry this message to alcoholics, and to practice these principles in all our affairs."

Finally, aware of who we are, we can let our light shine forth. The darkness of our character defects obscures our true selves. However, freely admitting our faults allows us to be ourselves without hiding in shame. Confident of our own essential goodness, we can act without fear. Instead of reacting defensively to perceived assaults, we can respond according to our chosen values, which reflect our true nature.

Nothing from outside can diminish who we are as a person. When my patients tell me how hurt they are at someone's disrespectful comment, I say, "Show me the hurt." They admit, "My pride was hurt." "Where is it? Show it to me," I urge them. Then, I ask, "Can anything anyone does to us affect the core of who we are? They may take your life, reputation, or possessions, but aren't we infinitely more than that?" In reality, it is not what others do to us that has lasting effect, but what we do to ourselves. Our own actions affect our core and have lasting, even eternal, consequences.

From a religious perspective, we get more than we deserve when we take full responsibility for our lives. When we sin, admit our guilt, and ask forgiveness, we are forgiven. We are not punished as we think we deserve, but we receive the free gift of God's mercy. Out of gratitude for all of our gifts from God, we seek to share from our abundance. We love as we have been loved first by God.

Social discourse today within our personal relationships and society, unfortunately, remains all too often deadlocked. We become entrenched into rigidly held positions of right and wrong, true and false, good and bad. We portray ourselves as innocent victims, while viewing our adversaries as guilty persecutors. We judge each other harshly. What can break this stalemate? Only a shift of perspective from focusing on our opponents to viewing ourselves with honesty and humility can turn the tide. Only by giving up the blaming and taking full personal responsibility for our own actions can we move forward. Then together we can seek the truth that will set us free.

CHAPTER TWENTY THREE

CROSS WORDS

"Father, into your hands I commend my spirit."
—Jesus of Nazareth

We Catholics aspire to take up our crosses daily and follow in Jesus' footsteps.

Marty and I are the old men in our workout group. Before class, we say, "I wonder what will hurt today?" Afterwards, exhausted, we joke, "It doesn't matter. Something will hurt, anyway." Our trainer encourages us to set goals for ourselves, to keep improving. I tell her, "My goal is to slow the slide." Marty and I are all too well aware that pain is inevitable with aging. The body just breaks down over time. Nothing can halt the decline.

"These are the times that try men's souls," wrote Thomas Paine, the American patriot. He wrote during the tumultuous period of the American Revolution while fighting the British. We are also living in a difficult time of transition. We are involved in cultural wars between different ideological groups. Families and relationships are torn apart by differing political opinions. The polarization is so deep, we refuse to talk about politics to keep the peace. Tragically, the differences of opinion often explode into violence, even against children. We bemoan, "It has never been this bad." Yet, a quick review of history shows we have never been immune from the pain of conflict and division. It's human nature.

A well-known piece of wisdom from the Buddhist tradition states, "Pain is inevitable; suffering is optional." What that epithet means is that by nature our bodies, the material world, and even society inevitably break down causing pain. How we react to that unavoidable pain determines how much we suffer mentally, emotionally, and spiritually. We suffer more when we resist that pain with unskillful means. We find relief when we learn to accept the pain with wisdom and courage. Ram Dass, the famous spiritual teacher, said, "Whatever happens in our life is there as a vehicle for transformation. Use it!"

We Christians believe in the inevitability of pain and suffering. Jesus said, "Unless the grain of wheat falls to the earth and dies, it remains just a grain of wheat. But if it dies it produces much fruit." He taught his disciples that they must be willing to deny themselves, take up their crosses, and follow in his footsteps. If they desire to preserve their life, they will lose it. Jesus underlined not just the inevitability but also the necessity of pain and suffering.

How are we to embrace this unavoidable pain of living in our world? How can we accept it with wisdom and courage? Is it possible even to find joy in our suffering?

JESUS' DYING WORDS

Jesus gave us an example in the way he suffered and died. He was an innocent man and died a humiliating execution on the cross like a common criminal. His words, as he hung between heaven and earth, reveal the meaning of his passion. His words point to how we can suffer wisely and well. His words are few, but powerful:

"My God, my God, why have you forsaken me?"

These are the only recorded words of Jesus on the cross in the oldest Gospels of Mark and Matthew. They shock us because they sound like words of despair. Actually, with these words Jesus is quoting the opening verse of Psalm 22. Jesus was a faithful Jew who knew well the Scriptures. He is calling on God in his distress to save him. It is a prayer of trust in God, not despair.

These words also indicate how deeply Jesus entered into his suffering. He did not reject or flee his cross of pain, but fully embraced it. Jesus did not diminish the physical, emotional, and spiritual agony that his crucifixion caused. He felt the pain of the scourging, crowning with thorns, and being nailed and hanged from the cross. He fully acknowledged his distress at being betrayed and abandoned by his closest friends and being mocked and humiliated by the crowd. He also expressed his sense of spiritual desolation at experiencing abandonment by God. Jesus did not deny, escape, or diminish the pain he felt. Without embracing it, he could not experience the joy of risen life.

"Father, forgive them; they do not know what they are doing."

According to Luke's account of the event, Jesus never saw himself as a helpless victim of a cruel persecutor. He never felt sorry for himself. As he was in the throes of death at the hands of his murderers, he did not become hostile and berate them. Instead, he looked upon them with compassion, as he had with all the people he encountered throughout his life. He asked that God forgive them. Further, he did not judge their intentions as malicious or evil. He recognized their ignorance of what they were doing and whom they were killing.

"I assure you: this day you will be with me in paradise."

Luke's Gospel also adds a conversation Jesus had with the two criminals crucified with him. He ignored the mocking of the one and praised the faith of the other. Even while suffering the agony of death, Jesus was not thinking of himself. He offered reassurance to his fellow sufferer. Jesus expressed his faith that life would overcome death. He knew from his intimacy with his Father that the delight of paradise, which he experienced daily, would continue after death.

"Father, into your hands I commend my spirit."

In Luke's Gospel, Jesus' final words were an offering of his life to his Father. Jesus' one goal in life was to obey the will of his Father and not his own. His life was one of total surrender in joy to his Father's will. He was God's beloved son and lived always in the presence of His love. The joy of loving motivated all he did. In the end, he died as he always lived—in complete surrender to the God of love. His death was a sacrificial offering of himself, just as was his daily life.

"Woman, there is your son....There is your mother."

John's Gospel adds the encounter of Jesus with his mother and his beloved disciple who stood at the foot of the cross. Two other Marys mourned there. All his other disciples ran away in fear. Again, even in all his pain, Jesus did not think about himself. His whole life was about bringing people together in faith, hope, and love. He meant his suffering and death to be a means of uniting all people. So, he invited his mother Mary and the beloved disciple to be a family, taking care of each other. This joining of his loved ones foreshadowed the Church, which was intended to be the community of God's beloved.

"I am thirsty."

Only John's Gospel includes these words. All the Gospels recount how the soldiers offered Jesus wine to numb the pain. Jesus refused. He wanted to be fully awake in his last moments. Jesus was never hungry or thirsty for anything to satisfy his physical needs. He refused to turn the stones to bread in the desert when the devil tempted him. He also did not honor the woman's request at the well in Samaria for an endless supply of water. Instead, he offered her the living water of eternal life. As in life, so in death, his hunger and thirst were always for God's word and to do His will.

"Now it is finished."

In John's Gospel, Jesus' final words were of his completion of his mission in life. He had devoted his life to doing God's work, and now his job was done. He felt a sense of fulfillment, not resignation, in his last moment. However, only one phase of Jesus' work was finished. Death was not an end. It was a new beginning of his work in the world. He promised his disciples the gift of his Spirit of truth and love. He also promised that he would be with them until the end of time.

JOYFUL SUFFERING

As we take up our crosses daily, what should our attitude be? We normally think that joy and suffering are opposites, never to be reconciled. However, the example of Jesus on the cross points the way to a path of reconciliation. We may learn:

Acceptance:

Life is so painful because it is an endless series of attachments and losses. Time is a thief. We invariably lose who and what we hold dear. Elizabeth Kubler-Ross famously described the five stages of grief that end in acceptance of the loss. We struggle through periods of denial, depression, anger, and bargaining before we accept the reality of the loss. Like Jesus, we cannot minimize the inevitable deep sufferings of life to heal. We need to embrace the totality of our distress, walk through the suffering, not around it. What we deny does not disappear, but only grows in intensity to erupt later with a vengeance.

Mary is my model of openness to whatever comes. I often repeat to myself her response to the Angel Gabriel: "I am the servant of the Lord.

Let it be done to me as you say." I ask God each morning: "What do you want of me today?"

Forgiveness:

We are both sinners and saints at the same time. We fail often, and others disappoint us. Jesus showed us that without mercy there is no hope. Suffering at the hands of others can either make us bitter or better. It can open or seal up our hearts. Replacing the anger and desire for revenge against those who harm us with forgiveness will set us free to love more deeply. Further, we often fail to live up to our own standards and can become prisoners of guilt. We also need to extend forgiveness and compassion to ourselves.

In an effort to pray unceasingly, as St. Paul urged, I repeat often during the day the Jesus Prayer, also called the Prayer of the Heart: "Lord Jesus Christ, Son of the living God, have mercy on me, a sinner."

Hope:

Despair is a close companion of inescapable distress. We can easily withdraw into self-pity and feel like a helpless victim, blaming others for our misery. Instead, Jesus demonstrated another way filled with a joyful hope. We too can accept our suffering as a path to new life. In doing so, we affirm our belief that life is stronger than death, that love overcomes hatred. Paradise awaits us not only later, but now, if we embrace our woundedness with hope.

I also frequently sing to myself the words of the Psalmist: "I place all my trust in you, my God; all my hope is in your mercy."

Self-Surrender:

In suffering, we tend to cling to our wounds. We can even identify with them and see ourselves as irreparably damaged. We may even view them as punishments from God for our sins. Jesus accepted his passion and death as a consequence of his obedience to God's will. His mission was to reveal God's word of love, to which many responded with hatred. In his death, as in his life, he surrendered himself into the loving hands of his Father. In the same way, we can offer up our sufferings for the benefit of others and ourselves. Our anguish can be our pleasing sacrifice in worshipping God.

I begin each day with the Morning Offering: "I offer You this day all my thoughts, works, joys, and sufferings."

Reconciliation:

Afflictions can easily make us bitter and self-centered. We blame others, seeing them as our persecutors. Our pain causes division, drives us apart from one another. Yet, Jesus revealed the gift of tears and the power of compassion. In his trials he felt kindness for others. Our suffering too can inspire compassion in others to care for us. It can also open our hearts to the sorrows of those around us and motivate us to reach out to them. Like Jesus, our suffering can be the means of bringing people together in mutual concern. In doing so, we become wounded healers, like Jesus.

Again, Mary is my model of creating family. I reflect on her words visiting her pregnant cousin Elizabeth: "My being proclaims the greatness of the Lord, my spirit finds joy in God my savior."

Deep Longings:

Two things cause our misery. Either we do not get what we want, or we get what we don't want. Jesus on the cross shows us that we need to attend to our deepest, not our superficial, longings. Pain makes us long for what is missing in our lives. Adversity also teaches us that we often hunger and thirst for what will never bring us lasting satisfaction. We may cling to our possessions, our health, our reputation, or even our relationships. We seek our happiness in things that pass. We suffer when we eventually, inevitably lose them. Our trials can be our teachers, calling us to seek lasting treasures. Our true happiness will come only from desiring and doing only what God wants of us. His will is for us to cultivate our true selves made in His image and flourish.

I often meditate on Jesus' Gethsemane Garden prayer: "Father, if it is your will, take this cup from me; yet not my will but yours be done."

New Beginnings:

We may fear that our sorrows will never end. Worse, we may suspect our strenuous efforts do not serve any useful purpose. However, Jesus' death was not in vain, only the end of his physical work. It launched a new beginning for the Church with the sending of the Spirit. Likewise, our struggles are not an end in themselves. Trials are unavoidable if we take seriously our mission to follow in the footsteps of Jesus. United with his sufferings, though, they have a deeper meaning. We only plant seeds. And no seed ever sees its flower. We may never see the fruits of our efforts, but we are assured that new life will blossom through God's grace.

Praying the Lord's Prayer reflectively gives me confidence: "Your kingdom come, your will be done, on earth as it is in heaven."

In conclusion, Vicktor Frankl, the German psychologist and Holocaust survivor, famously said, "Those who have a 'why' to live, can bear with almost any 'how'." If we cannot find meaning in the inevitable pains of living, we will fall into despair. However, if we suffer for a cause greater than ourselves, we can bear it. Jesus showed us by the way he lived and died, embracing his cross, that if we dedicate ourselves to the highest cause, to serving God's will, we can overcome our suffering. In fact, we can even find joy in our trials.

CHAPTER TWENTY FOUR

EVERYTHING IS GRACE

"You are with me always, and everything I have is yours."
—Luke 15: 31

We Catholics believe marriage is a sacrament, a reflection of Christ's love of His Church.

"I'll never get married again!" a patient of mine affirmed. She had gone through a bitter divorce and had begun dating. Many of her dates had been disappointing. I asked her about her experience with men. She said, "I keep giving and giving but don't get much in return. Love relationships are not a good bargain." She saw herself as a person with much to give but who had been let down in love. She admitted looking for a return on her emotional investment in romantic relationships. The men in her life just had not measured up to her expectations.

A romantic view of relationships prevails in our society. We have high expectations of love. Adele expresses our high expectations and disappointment when she sings, "We could have had it all." We look for our soulmate, our perfect match. Many of us enter relationships with the hope that the other person will complete us, make us happy.

However, when our partners do not live up to our expectations, we become disillusioned and resentful. "I didn't bargain for this," we tell ourselves. Then, we move on—often again and again.

Such high romantic hopes may underlie much of the current instability in marriage and reluctance to make life-long commitments we observe today. What assumptions underlie these high expectations? Is there another way to view relationships that can offer lasting peace and growth?

PARABLES OF GROWTH

Three parables offer contrasting views about the nature of relationships, both with God and with one another:

Parable of the Seed

In this familiar parable recounted in the first three Gospels (Mark 4: 1-20), a farmer goes out to sow seeds in his field. The seeds fall on different soils and produced various yields. They fall on the footpath, on rocky ground, among thorns, and on good soil. Jesus interprets the parable as different ways we receive the seed of God's word. Those who open their hearts to hear God's message, those with good soil, yield an extravagant harvest.

Initially, the parable appears to focus on the various ways we are open or closed to God's word of love. It is about what kind of ground we cultivate within our hearts to receive His love, about the efforts we make. It is then a parable about seeds and soils. However, a deeper reading focuses on what is truly surprising in the story. The sower scatters the seed with extravagance, no matter the soil. And it produces a wondrous harvest up to a hundred-fold. From this perspective, the parable is really about the extravagant generosity of the sower, who is God. It is more about what God does for us than what we do for Him. His love is extended to all without judgment and produces abundant fruit in our lives.

Parable of the Laborers

In this parable (Matthew 20: 1-16), the owner of an estate goes out into the marketplace to hire workers for his vineyard. He goes out at different times of the day and promises them the usual wage. At the end of the day, he pays all the workers the same amount, as he promised, no matter how many hours they worked. Naturally, those who worked longer, bearing the heat of the day, expected a greater payment and protested. We understand well their outrage at the perceived injustice. In their minds, they deserved to be paid more. We also believe that we should be rewarded according to our efforts. The harder we work, the more we should prosper. That is how our American marketplace works.

The parable ends with a stinger which reveals its true meaning. This story overturns our natural standards of justice and entitlement. The owner reminds the workers that they were paid a just wage, as they had agreed. However, to our surprise, the owner, who represents God, proclaims his free generosity. He can give any of us more than we deserve, according to His wishes. This is a parable about the limits of our ideas of justice in the face of God's abundant generosity.

Parable of the Prodigal Son

In this well-known parable (Luke 15: 11-32), a son asks his father for his inheritance, wanders off, and squanders it. When he realizes his misery, he repents and returns home. His father awaits him and throws a party upon his return. The older son refuses to celebrate. He argues, reasonably, that he has always been faithful and never received special recognition. Violating his sense of justice, he protested that the wayward son received the honor he himself deserved.

At first glance, the parable may appear to be about the repentance of a son who was forgiven and the jealousy of the hardworking, faithful son. However, it is really about the extravagant mercy of the father. He overlooks his younger son's misdeeds and reminds his older son of his constant love. He says, "You are with me always, and everything I have is yours." The merciful father, representing God, reminds us of his continuous love, no matter what we do. His mercy overlooks our faults.

PERSONAL ACCOUNTING SYSTEM

These parables underline two distinct patterns of relationship. In the first, the less mature, relationships are governed by a personal accounting system. In the second, the more mature, everything is grace, a free gift, in loving relationships.

Our culture promotes the first view. We engage in relationships with many expectations, some of which are blatantly unrealistic. Or course, we cannot avoid having expectations when we engage with others. We tell each other honestly what we would like. However, if we hold our expectations too tightly, they become demands, rather than requests. We do not respect the freedom of our partners to refuse to indulge our desires or to address them in their own ways.

Our culture promotes a sense of entitlement in pursuing what we want. It encourages us to want more and more to the point we may say to ourselves, "I want it all, and I want it now." Similarly, we pursue a romantic ideal in our loving relationships, which can take on a near-religious aura. "People who need people are the luckiest people in the world," Barbra Streisand sings and we proclaim. We believe that intimate relationships are the privileged path to happiness and ultimate fulfillment. Furthermore, we believe that couples marry to make each other happy. In so doing, however, we place the burden of our happiness in the hands of our partner.

This romantic view shapes the way we think about love, ourselves, and our partners. We desire to be worthy in love and seek worthy partners. Love must be earned by our caring behavior and be returned in kind. We may give freely but expect to get love in return. We believe we are entitled to be happy in our relationships and seek "the right person" who will fulfill that need. We also feel responsible to make our partners happy and hope they feel the same way about us. Our contentment resides in the happiness of our partner.

In our interactions, we develop a personal accounting system. We may have expectations, some explicit and others implicit, about how we want to be treated. At its worst, despite the professed idealism, our relationships may degenerate into an impersonal business arrangement, an assessment of our partner's assets and liabilities. Our expectations express our wishes for how we wish our partners to be and behave. When they do not measure up to our expectations, we become disappointed and resentful. As the AA saying states, "The road to resentment is paved by expectation." We may wish our partners to be different when their character faults reveal themselves. When they do not change as we wish, we may withdraw in frustration.

Beneath this apparently idealistic view of relationships is a hidden focus on our personal deficiency. We tell ourselves, "I need you and can't live without you." Relationships are need-driven, based on the sense that we are incomplete in ourselves. Our partner fills a void in our lives. The other fulfills and completes us. We may fear being alone. Without the other we would be lonely and miserable.

This pattern of relating also shapes our relationship with God. We see ourselves as sinners deserving of punishment. We strive to keep all the commandments to prove ourselves worthy of God's love. We expect to be rewarded for virtue and punished for our vices. However, we live in constant fear of not measuring up to God's standards.

EVERYTHING IS GRACE

In the second view of relationships expressed in the parables, all is God's grace. Relationships are not our primary path to happiness, but a grace-filled means to personal growth. Joseph Campbell, the expert on the psychology of myths, expressed this alternative view directly: "I think one of the problems in marriage is that people don't realize what it is. They think it's a long love affair and it isn't. Marriage has nothing to do with being happy. It has to do with being transformed, and when the transformation is realized it is a magnificent experience. But you have to submit. You have to yield. You have to give. You can't dictate." (1)

We cannot expect our partner to make us happy. Naturally, we ask for what we want, but do not become demanding. We listen with openness to their deepest desires. However, happiness is an inside job, our personal responsibility. It depends on our own efforts to live according to our own highest standards, to be loving and generous with others. The best gift we can give to our partner is our best self. The relationship is an arena that challenges us to confront our character defects and love whole-heartedly. It is a crucible to develop character. The interactions with our partner are like a magnifying glass that exposes who we really are and where we need to improve. We will be happy only when we live out of our true selves and according to our deepest desires.

Viewing relationships as an opportunity for personal growth shapes our views of love, ourselves, and others. Loving and being loved is a free gift that cannot be earned, coerced, or controlled. Forced love is bondage. Authentic love is giving without expecting a return. It is about giving whole-heartedly and not about getting back. We see ourselves as beloved individuals who want to share our life and love with our partner. We respect the otherness of our partners, appreciating them as they are, and not as we wish them to be. We acknowledge the strengths and weaknesses in ourselves and our partners, so we can treat each other with kindness and mercy. Without forgiveness, no relationship can last.

This grace-filled view of relationships is based on abundance thinking. We tell each other, "I have much to give and want to share my life with you." We appreciate the goodness within ourselves and our partners despite the character flaws. We see us as made in the image and likeness of God. In our interactions, we allow God's love that fills our hearts to overflow. Gratitude and joy, rather than bitterness and resentment, shape our interactions, even in difficult times. In our relationships, we live out the Sufi saying, "I was a hidden treasure and loved to be known."

Viewing everything as grace, a free gift, changes how we relate to God. We believe in the extravagant generosity of God, even in our failings. He is for us a God of Love who constantly seeks to be close to us. In fact, He dwells in our hearts. Because of our faith in His mercy and forgiveness, there is no room for fear. We have nothing to prove. Instead, we live with joy and cheerfulness, seeking a closer union with our Beloved.

GRACEFUL RELATIONSHIPS

The cultural messages about relationships are powerful and seductive. How can we challenge these distorted views? How can we enlarge our personal views about intimacy? How can we begin to cultivate graceful relationships? I suggest these practices:

Gratitude

When we have high expectations of our partner, we set ourselves up for disappointment. Inevitably, our partner will fail and not live up to our standards. We then become preoccupied with what is missing in the relationship. A shift in attention can remedy this heartache. We can focus on all the good things we have received in our life. What do we have that was not given to us? Our very life, our capacity and desire for love, our partner's love, and so forth. Our gratitude inspires spontaneous generosity to share with others from the abundance we have received.

Freedom

Our expectations become a mental prison for ourselves and our partners. We give love only when our partner lives up to our standards. Our love becomes conditional. We demand that others be as we wish them to be. The way out of this prison is to follow the advice of the Buddhist monk Thich Nhat Hahn, "Love the other in a way that makes them feel free." Genuine love can only be freely given and received. We show that mature love when both partners can honestly say to each other, "I leave you free to be yourself, to think your own thoughts, to pursue your own interests, to behave in any way that suits you." We then remove the conditions and limits we place on loving. Then, both of us in the relationship are free to be our true selves.

No-Strings Love

If our love arises from a sense of personal justice, we will only give if we have the assurance of an equal and similar return from our partner. The shadow of disappointment and the withholding of love are not far away, opening the door to resentment. Our anger then breeds a similar response in our partner. We can escape this painful dilemma by freely and generously giving our love without counting the cost. We love others out of the abundance of the goodness within us which we desire to share. We love because that is who we are. That is our path to genuine happiness. By loving wholeheartedly we will be surprised at the impact it has on our partner. He or she will be drawn to us and more inclined to freely give in return.

Embrace Differences

When we hold our partners prisoners of our expectations, we give them the message that we will accept them only if they conform to our image of how they should be. Often, we expect them to react, think, and behave just like us—be our clones. This narrow view of the other as an extension of ourselves destroys the possibility of enrichment and growth in the relationship. Our partner's otherness shakes us out of our complacency, inviting us to expand our consciousness and open our hearts. Furthermore, as much as we may hate confrontation, we need conflict to grow. If everything goes along as we wish, nothing changes.

We stagnate and continue to live in our self-centered worlds. The conflicts cause us to look inward and reassess our lives and relationship.

Communication

When we feel bad about ourselves, we look for assurance from others to build up our self-esteem. We also fear exposing ourselves. Honest communication, the foundation of any marriage, begins with a healthy appreciation of our own goodness and uniqueness. We cannot be any more intimate or loving with another than we are with ourselves. We want our partners to know us, and we want to know them in depth. So, we share with each other our own unique truth, or most intimate thoughts and feelings. It is most helpful to begin our intimate conversations with "I statements," inviting our partner into our hearts and minds. We avoid the "you statements" that often express our judgments of the other.

Forgiveness

When we regularly judge our partners, we begin to focus more and more on their faults and what is missing in our relationship. We overlook their goodness, ignoring the reasons that brought us together. In reality, we are all both saints and sinners, holy and flawed. If we can come to forgive our imperfections, we can begin to forgive our partners for theirs. Misunderstandings and failings are inevitable in any relationship. If accepted with understanding and mercy, they can be a path to growth and intimacy.

It should be noted that forgiveness does not always demand reconciliation. We are not obligated to tolerate the intolerable. We have a duty to protect ourselves in the face of profound abuse or neglect. We can forgive, release the anger, but choose not to remain in the harmful relationship.

Marriage and committed relationship are unsettled these days. They do not provide the security they once did. Nevertheless, despite our repeated disappointments, we continue to maintain high expectations that the love of our significant other will bring us lasting happiness. However, a shift in perspective can renew our hope for joy in loving. Relationships are not intended to make us happy. Instead, the challenges of relating to those closest to us can help us grow in mature love. Our intimate relationships provide the best arena for personal growth. They expose our hidden faults and invite us to be generous, honest, and forgiving. We learn to give and receive love freely and unconditionally, just as God has shown us.

CHAPTER TWENTY FIVE

SOUNDS OF SILENCE

"Be still and know that I am God."
—Psalm 46: 10

We Catholics believe God speaks to us in the silence of prayer, meditation, and contemplation.

At the end of therapy sessions, my patients often ask me, "What can I do to make this better? Can you give me an exercise?" My advice is always the same, which mostly disconcerts them, "Just pay close attention to yourself." "How do I do that?" they ask. "Just be quiet, listen, and see what you learn about yourself," I respond. I explain, "You can only heal from the inside out. When you understand yourself, you will know what to do."

My patients see themselves as broken and needing to be fixed. They view me as the expert who will guide them to health. It is as if they are a broken car, and I am a skilled mechanic. They want a manual of repairs for a quick fix. I tell them, "You have the answer within you, but may not know it yet."

We live in an attention deficit culture. We are hyperactive and need to keep busy. Being alone and quiet makes us restless and nervous. We are easily distracted. Quickly bored, we need near-constant stimulation. We are also impatient and want quick and easy answers to our problems. Problem-solving comes naturally. We like to fix things. We believe that there is a solution to every problem, if we just take the right approach.

However, the approach our culture trains us to take keeps us on the surface of our lives. We think we can manipulate our psyches like we repair the kitchen sink. However, we are not objects that can be so easily controlled. We are flesh and blood human beings with a soul.

These days, in the wake of the pandemic, the numbers of those suffering from anxiety and depression, substance abuse, domestic violence, and suicide have soared. Current research indicates that nearly a third of adolescents and adults experience clinical levels of anxiety and depression. Further, our wounds run deep to the core of who we are. We also suffer spiritual desolation and despair about the meaning of our lives. We lack balance and clear direction. The old answers no longer satisfy us. Commenting on modern society, the poet William Butler Yeats wrote, "Things fall apart; the center cannot hold."

How can we heal our wounded psyches? How can we find our center and keep our balance? How can we recover our souls?

AN INSIDE JOB

We tend to live on the surface of our lives, in an arid flatland. When problems occur and we feel stressed, we look for immediate solutions in two ways. Our first instinct is to look outside ourselves to find the cause of our troubles—a job loss, a broken relationship, failing health. We then put our energy into changing the disturbing situation. In the process, we try to stay strong, "fake it until we make it."

In this outside-in approach to problem-solving, we imagine that healing and happiness come from creating more favorable life circumstances. We tell ourselves we will feel better when we get what we want and get rid of what we dislike. We work hard to change our outer lives. When we meet resistance in our attempts to control the uncontrollable outer world and others, we may feel frustrated. We may keep pushing ourselves to the point of exhaustion, or give up in despairing resignation.

Healing and growth can occur only when we shift our focus from the outside to our inner selves. It is not the circumstances of our lives, which are always changing, that make us either happy or miserable. Our inner attitude, our state of mind, toward what happens to us determines our wellbeing. Notice how differently people react to the same situation. Some people get better, while others become bitter. A close observation of our own reactions reveals the truth of what Tilopa, the renowned Buddhist teacher, says, "It is not the outer objects that entangle us. It is the inner clinging that entangles us."

Our second approach to healing is to get rid of the distressing feelings— the anger, sadness, or anxiety—as quickly as we can. We view these uncomfortable feelings as the obstacles to our wellbeing. So we devise many strategies to escape their grip. We may deny these feelings and just press on regardless. Or we may keep ourselves busy and distracted so we do not notice them. Or we may medicate ourselves with alcohol, drugs, food, or a variety of addictive activities.

All these strategies are in the service of avoiding pain. They work in the short run, but eventually wear us out. It is like chasing our shadow, making us only exhausted. It takes enormous energy to keep our emotions underground. In fact, all these suppressed feelings grow in intensity when buried. They enslave us. They also seep out indirectly in our behaviors and attitudes. Finally, they may emerge fully in a psychological disorder, which is the return of the repressed.

I tell my weary patients, "What you consider the problem is really only a symptom. You have to dig deep within yourself to discover the root cause." For example, when we experience some physical pain, like a stomachache, we do not know how to treat it until we know the cause. A diagnostic examination is needed. If it is caused by indigestion, the treatment is far different than if it is caused by stomach cancer.

Similarly, our psychological suffering is a symptom that directs our attention to the underlying cause. Something neglected within us is crying out to be noticed. The work of therapy is to expose the roots of our distress. Only then can we pursue effective strategies of relief. Accurate self-awareness leads to healing and growth. So, I encourage my patients, "Just sit with those uncomfortable feelings and thoughts to see what you can learn about yourself. What is the message of your distress?"

How do we sit with our reactions and learn from them?

JUST SIT

Socrates taught, "The unexamined life is not worth living." He invited his followers to be quiet and reflect deeply on their lives. He promised that they would discover the truth that would set them free.

We begin this personal self-examination by simply being alone and quiet with ourselves. That can be a new and frightening experience for many of us who drive ourselves to keep busy and productive. We are more comfortable in the outer world than with our inner experience. Looking inward, we encounter darkness, some light, and much mystery. The unknown frightens us.

I invite my patients to become observers of themselves. I explain that their consciousness is like a free-flowing river of thoughts, feelings, and reactions. It never stops. We can try to block its flow with great effort, but eventually the dam breaks. Or we can just jump into the river and be carried away by our thoughts and feelings, eventually drowning in them. What I propose is a third alternative. I invite my patients to stand back and observe themselves carefully. I invite them to pay close attention to their reactions in the various situations in their lives.

When my patients make the time and effort to observe themselves, they begin to notice how all their reactions come and go and do not belong to them. They also hear the inner dialogue, the storytelling, that goes on constantly in their minds. I tell them, "Your feelings last only last 90 seconds. What intensifies and prolongs them are the stories you tell yourself." Over time, they recognize patterns in their stories that generate their misery. They learn how they identified with the distorted messages they received from childhood and society. For example, many keep telling themselves they are not good enough, are losers, and can do nothing right. The obvious consequence of such thinking is a depressed and anxious mood.

Healing and growth occur as we become more aware of our distorted thinking and reacting, challenge them, and become more attuned to present day reality.

When we become more adept at observing ourselves, we can look more deeply into the flow of our consciousness. We become aware of a mysterious Source within us, which is the wellspring of our healing and growth. We glimpse our soul, our inner spirit, which contains an untapped wisdom, energy, and delight. In religious terms, we may call it the Divine Life within us.

We experience this subtle, hidden Source by just sitting and being quiet with ourselves. We turn off the chattering mind (called the wild monkey mind), not giving our thoughts attention and energy, and listen with our hearts. I define prayer, meditation, and contemplation as simply paying full attention to the present moment, not getting lost in distracting thoughts. If we do not risk being alone with ourselves, we will miss this depth and continue to live on the surface of our lives. The misery-go-round will keep going.

The *Tao Te Ching* (16) expresses beautifully the experience and consequences of just sitting and listening with the heart:

Empty your mind of all thoughts.

Let your heart be at peace.

Watch the turmoil of beings,

but contemplate their return.

Each separate being in the universe

returns to the common source.

Returning to the source is serenity.

If you don't realize the source,

you stumble in confusion and sorrow.

When you realize where you come from,

you naturally become tolerant,

disinterested, amused,

kindhearted as a grandmother,

dignified as a king.

Returning to the source, to the Divine Life within us, is the antidote to our spiritual malaise. We embrace the wisdom, energy, and joy to live a full and meaningful life.

SITTING PRACTICE

Let me suggest a way of entering the silence within us and listening to its life-giving sounds. I tell my patients, "Stop and do nothing." They tell me doing nothing is the hardest thing for them to do. That is no surprise. We define ourselves by what we do. Our self-esteem depends on our being constantly busy and productive. We are preoccupied with fixing ourselves, making ourselves better.

The recommendation to stop and do nothing is an invitation to relax with ourselves as we are in the moment. We begin by being alone and quiet. We may just sit or walk leisurely, with our minds focused on our inner experience. Thoughts and reactions arise unavoidably. We just notice them and let them go. We get into trouble when we cling to our thoughts and put all our faith in their truthfulness. Something is not true just because we think it. Our thoughts, feelings, and reactions are like clouds in the sky with little real substance. We gently watch them pass. Our consciousness is the vast blue sky that remains and watches.

It can be helpful to attend to our experience, and not our thoughts, by focusing on some object. Some focus on their breath, a lighted candle, or a favorite phrase. I focus on the phrase, "Be still and know that I am God." That thought engages my attention and calms me. When competing thoughts arise, I return to the phrase. We can only think of one thing at a time. I have to do this over and over in my quiet time. It takes much practice to let go of our thoughts and maintain our concentration.

As we enter into the silence and stillness, serenity will overtake us. We rest in the simple feeling of being. We are freed from the compulsion to do anything. We experience the miracle of being alive and are filled with gratitude. All is a gift, not earned. We sense that everything is perfect deep down, as it should be. We are not as broken as we imagine, needing to be fixed. We also relax in the spaciousness of our mind.

There we connect with our inner wisdom, courage, and joy of being alive.

In short, through this time alone with ourselves we find our center. Like a gyroscope in our fast-moving lives, it will provide balance. During these quiet moments we cultivate trust in our higher consciousness, in our wise mind. When we return to our daily tasks, we are more alert and aware. We can observe all the disturbing thoughts and feelings that inevitably arise with a sense of calm. Then, we can engage our wise minds to make sense of the chaos of our emotional reactions and distorted thoughts. When we feel overwhelmed, we can return to our quiet inner place to be refreshed.

We live in a hyperactive culture, driven to keep busy and productive. As a consequence, we live on the surface of life, tossed about by the waves of circumstances and our emotional reactions. We will only find serenity, healing, and growth if we enter into the depths of our inner life. Spending time alone with ourselves we discover a Higher Consciousness, a Divine Presence, in the silence. Those silent moments can become the inexhaustible wellspring for creating a full and creative life for ourselves and others.

CHAPTER TWENTY SIX

RESPECT

"All I'm askin' is for a little respect when you come home."
—Aretha Franklin

We Catholics believe in the dignity of every human being.

"I can't believe how my coworker disrespected me," an angry patient exclaimed. She explained that her colleague publicly criticized her work at a meeting. "What nerve she had! I'm one of the most competent workers in my department," she added. My patient admitted that her critic did not call her any names or question her abilities. Nevertheless, she felt personally attacked. I wondered what was at stake for my patient in the questioning of her performance.

Another patient of mine became uncomfortable when I complimented him. He said, "I never trust compliments. I always wonder what someone wants from me when they praise me." When we explored his reaction, he admitted, "I see myself as a loser and can't believe the good things people say about me." He clearly lacked self-respect.

In both cases, whether criticized or praised, my patients did not feel appreciated for how they saw themselves. Respect for them was a validation of their own self-image, whether positive or negative.

RESPECTFUL LOOKING

According to the dictionary, the word respect means "to admire someone or something deeply, as a result of their abilities, qualities, or achievements." The word comes from the Latin "re + specere," which means "to look again, to take a second look." We look at both others and ourselves with respectful eyes.

All of us want to be respected, especially by our loved ones. We want to be appreciated for who we are and what we do. Our self-esteem often depends on what people say and think about us. Our moods may rise and fall according to how others react to us. We want respect and to be treated respectfully. The words of Aretha Franklin's classic song "Respect" resonate with us, "All I'm askin' is for a little respect when you come home."

Most important, however, we want to respect ourselves. How we see ourselves overflows in our viewing of others. We all have an idea of who we are and how we want to live. Our self-esteem depends on the degree we live up to our expectations of ourselves. In the end, we (and God), not others, are the most significant judges of our lives. Invariably, our self-judgment becomes projected onto others.

Our preoccupation with respect reveals confusion about precisely what that word means for us. Do we want to be appreciated, by ourselves and others, for who we really are or for who we imagine ourselves to be? Do we want to be admired for our real or pretended accomplishments? Does real respect recognize our true value or just our imagined worth. The two views are not the same. Our self-image, what we think about ourselves, is not the same as our true self, which can be a mystery. That mystery may take a lifetime of effort to plumb.

The word respect, a looking again, expresses this ambiguity. It suggests that there are two different ways of seeing—a first and a second glance. The first glance is based on a superficial impression, while the second takes a deeper look into our true nature. Likewise, our self-esteem can be rooted in either viewing, on appearance or reality.

THE FIRST GLANCE

In assessing ourselves and others, the first look is based on superficial appearances. We focus on first impressions of how others present themselves and on our own initial reactions. All of us wear a social mask. We want to put our best foot forward in order to be accepted. Whether we feel respected or not then depends on the degree to which that image is accepted or rejected by others. We also engage in a constant silent inner assessment of how we appear to others.

Our first glance is never unbiased. We entertain standards, sometimes explicit, but mostly implicit, of how we expect ourselves and others to behave. These expectations develop over a lifetime, from messages we receive in childhood and from society. For example, we may believe we must always be successful and never show weakness; or that everyone must like us; or that we must earn love. We spontaneously judge ourselves and others by these standards. All too often, our expectations are colored by our self-interest. We approve of what appears to benefit us and disapprove what does not add value to us. We quickly praise and condemn, based on these limited views.

In reality, the first spontaneous glance is through the eyes of a child. All of us have unconscious infantile reactions to our world from time to time. Our childhood experiences of being powerless, helpless, and overwhelmed occasionally seep through our adult interactions. To compensate, children naturally develop a sense of infantile omnipotence. They see themselves as the center of the universe, causing everything around them to happen. They entertain grandiose ideas of themselves that translate into unrealistic expectations of themselves and others as they grow older. As adults we may see the world through the lens of our need to be special and admired for being extraordinary. We abhor being ordinary and average.

In assessing ourselves and others, we apply these idealistic expectations. Hidden desires about how we think the world ought to be possess us. Of course, we all inevitably fall short of these ideals. We then become condemning of ourselves and others. Our self-esteem is fragile, easily shattered. We feel disrespected for small matters, and others do not feel validated by us.

THE SECOND GLANCE

In observing ourselves and others, the second look seeks to know reality. It takes a long, hard look beneath the surface of appearances. We acknowledge our depth and the infinite mystery of who we are. No ideas or images can fully capture the richness of our personalities. We are humble making judgments about ourselves and others, aware of our limitations of understanding. We avoid making snap value judgments. We are open to learning more about ourselves and others, fascinated with the journey into the unknown.

The second glance attempts to be aware of our prejudices and to let them go. We seek to be all-inclusive in our perspective, searching for our underlying unity. We believe that we are all alike in sharing human nature, which is both flawed and glorious. In fact, we are all part of a wonderful universe, constantly interchanging with all its parts. We have a deep respect for ourselves, others, and all nature which comes from the same mysterious Life-Force and Intelligence. We are also devoted to the wellbeing of all because we know we share the same fate on this spaceship earth.

In our relationships with each other, we focus on both what we hold in common and what makes us unique. We all desire to be happy and to be free from suffering. We strive to see ourselves in others and to treat them the way we want to be treated. If we look deep enough, beneath all the flaws, we see our inherent dignity as children of God. We all reflect the glory of God's Presence in our own unique ways. At its deepest level, our caring for one another not only benefits all, but it is an offering of our lives to God. Jesus reminded us, "Whatever you do to the least of my brothers you do to me." (Matthew 25: 40)

The second glance is a look at others and ourselves with mature eyes. Deep down, we all want to be known and accepted as we truly are. Only the truth will set us free. Our illusions will only enslave us. So, we make the effort to know ourselves and others as we are, and not as we wish ourselves to be. We do not ask what others can do for us, but how we can love them more perfectly. We take full responsibility for our lives, striving to live according to our highest values. At the same time, we can accept weaknesses in ourselves and others, have compassion, and forgive. We work patiently for improvement.

In assessing ourselves and others, we do not entertain false expectations. We try to build each other up and not tear each other down with condemnation. Compassion for our shared humanity guides us. We look at each other with kindness and love. That is the essence of the second glance.

BECOMING RESPECTFUL

It takes a lifetime of effort to become deeply respectful of ourselves and others. Giving up our illusions about how we think ourselves and others should be does not come easy. W.H. Auden wrote: "We would rather be ruined than changed. We would rather die in our dread than climb the cross of the moment and let our illusions die." A death is required for new life to emerge. Here are some suggestions to prepare the ground for this personal transformation:

Be open to all experiences:

We all tend to be selective about our experiences. We welcome what is pleasant and shun what is painful. We find ways to protect ourselves from what causes us pain—all those uncomfortable and surprising thoughts, feelings, and reactions. If we follow our natural path of avoidance, we will remain stagnant. However, if we risk being willing to bear discomfort, we can begin to learn more about ourselves and grow. Pain is our teacher. Our suffering reveals that something is amiss and needs to be addressed. Pain is a cry for attention from deep within us. We need to be willing to sit with our suffering—the fears, anger, and sadness—to learn their message. Then we can know what we need to do to make our lives better.

Pay full attention:

We like to stay busy and be productive. That constant activity can keep us stuck on the surface of our lives. It can distract us from knowing who we really are. For healing and growth, we need to pay full attention to ourselves. That requires a willingness to be alone and quiet with ourselves. Any good friendship thrives when we spend quality time together and communicate who we really are. A neglected friendship fades. Similarly, we need to develop a friendly relationship with ourselves before we can have a close relationship with anyone else. We become intimate with ourselves, getting to know who we are at ever deeper levels. Of course, the deepest level is to discover our soul, the place of our communion with the Divine.

Make a daily personal examen—Naikan:

Growing up Catholic, I was taught to make an examination of conscience before every confession. I was also taught to examine myself each night before going to bed. That recommendation expressed a timeless wisdom. As Socrates said, "The unexamined life is not worth living."

Naikan, which is a Japanese method of self-reflection, provides a balanced way of stepping back and observing our lives. (Gregg Krech, *Naikan*, Berkeley: Stone Bridge Press, 2002) The word "naikan" means "looking inside." In making our personal examen we venture looking inside with an open mind and full attention to see what we discover. The practice suggests that we ask ourselves three questions at the end of each day:

What have I received from others? We ask ourselves what specific people have done for us during the last 24 hours. We acknowledge even the smallest gifts from others—a kind word, cooking a meal, washing our clothes. We become more aware of how we are dependent on others for our wellbeing in so many unacknowledged ways. The reflection inspires gratitude in us.

What have I given to others? We ask ourselves what we have specifically done that day to be helpful to others. Even the small gifts are important—listening to a friend, picking up trash, feeding the birds. We become more aware of how others depend on us. We also wake up to our responsibility to make the world a better place for all of us.

What troubles and difficulties have I caused others? We humbly and honestly admit to ourselves how we have failed, even in small ways—an unkind thought or word, gossiping, ignoring my wife. This personal confession can inspire remorse and the firm purpose to amend our lives. Of course, we do not have to dwell on our faults. We acknowledge them, find ways of correcting them, and ask God for forgiveness. Sometimes, the most difficult task is then to forgive ourselves.

Welcome criticism:

We ordinarily love praise and hate criticism. We often take any criticism as a personal attack on us without examining its merit. However, we learn more about ourselves from being corrected than from being honored. "Rebuke a wise man, and he will love you," the wisdom teacher exclaimed. Our critics are our best teachers. When we stop and think about it, how is criticism ever harmful, if we are willing to listen with an open mind and look honestly at ourselves? If the correction is accurate, it may reveal a fault that eludes us. Then we can be grateful to the critic for his feedback. If the critical remark is inaccurate, we can just ignore it. In the end, nothing that anyone thinks, says, or does to us can touch the core of who we are. We are the captains of our souls, the masters of our own fate. Actually, it is only what we think, say, and do that helps or harms us, depending on whether or not we are living up to our highest values.

We live in a culture that values self-image and demands respect. We are driven to be successful and look good. These aspirations set us up to feeling easily insulted. We often strive to live up to standards that are impossible. We focus on how we miss the mark, and then suffer low self-esteem. However, real respect recognizes our true value, and not merely our imagined worth. If we make the effort to take a close second look at ourselves we can set ourselves free to love. If we come to know and accept ourselves as the flawed and dignified human being we are, we can treat each other with genuine respect and compassion.

CHAPTER TWENTY SEVEN

LIFE'S JOY

"What can separate us from the love of Christ?"
—Paul of Tarsus

We Catholics believe God made us to know, love, and serve Him and be happy with Him on earth and in heaven.

"I've never been happy. I don't believe I'll ever escape my misery," my elderly patient lamented. She had suffered from anxiety her whole life. She was its prisoner. "I'm always worrying about something. If it's not one thing, it's another. Anything can cause me to panic," she explained. I asked her, "Who would you be if you didn't worry?" She responded honestly, "I don't know. I wouldn't know myself. That would be even scarier!" My patient had constructed an identity around her illness. She could not imagine living without it and the misery it caused her.

Another patient of mine was terrified of leaving the house. She insisted she wanted to feel free to go out and socialize but still stayed home to feel safe. I asked her, "You say you want to go out, but still stay home. Which is true, what you say you want or what you do?" Both, in fact, may have been true. She felt hopelessly conflicted, not knowing what she really wanted for herself. She saw herself trapped in miserable indecision.

After 30 years of practicing psychology, I have come to this shocking conclusion: many people love their illnesses. They live as if addicted to their misery. They complain about their physical, emotional, and mental suffering, but seem to cling to it for dear life. Consciously, they hate their painful conditions, but I suspect that secretly, perhaps unknown to them, they love them. For them to change and let go of their fears, sadness, or anger would be terrifying. They identify with their wounded states that restrict their lives. The familiarity gives them comfort. To venture out from the protective walls of their illnesses would take them into unknown territory. They would have to take full responsibility for their lives in pursuing their deepest values.

I often ask my patients, "What would you do if you were not so depressed or anxious?" Some confess they don't know. They live at a distance from their own desires. Others give me a list of things they would like to do. I then ask, "What keeps you from doing what you want?" They respond, "My emotional state." I challenge them, "Why do you give your moods so much power over your life?" I wonder to myself if giving in to the moods is easier than pushing themselves to pursue their values. Their illnesses give them an excuse not to engage fully in life.

When we suffer deeply from physical, emotional, or mental problems, we may feel powerless. We come to believe that misery is our natural state. The Buddha taught that the first noble truth is that life is suffering. Jesus commanded his disciples to take up their crosses and follow him. That suffering is an inescapable experience of life needs no proof.

But is misery our natural state? Or are we born to be happy? Since suffering is unavoidable, is it possible to find joy in it? Where do we find a lasting joy in life?

RELIGION'S RESPONSE

The best teachers of religion are the community of believers, not the official ordained ministers who proclaim doctrines. Those in the pew teach by how they live and give an accounting of their faith. What kind of faith does the average believer profess? Do they demonstrate by their lives and attitudes that we were created by God to be happy here and now, or only in the afterlife?

Nearly all Americans report that they believe in God (92%), even though an increasing number are not affiliated with any church. They label themselves more spiritual than religious. What kind of God do most of us believe in? According to research, God has many different faces for us. Nearly a third (31%) professes faith in an Authoritarian God who is a wrathful, sin-hating deity. He rewards good deeds and punishes evil acts. Nearly a quarter of Americans (24%) view God as distant, residing in heaven. He is the uninvolved creative force behind and above the natural universe. Sixteen percent believe in a Critical God who monitors us closely, enforces His justice, and makes everything right at the end of the world. Another quarter (23%) trusts in a Benevolent God of mercy, who forgives sinners and brings peace to the world. (1)

It is noteworthy that the vast majority of us (77%) have a more negative than positive view of God. He is a God who inspires more fear than love. This God scrutinizes, judges, or stands aloof. Our view of God translates into how we behave as His believers. We see ourselves as made in His image and likeness. Many of us believers, then, become watch guards and harsh judges of ourselves and others, or we withdraw from this corrupt world. We are preoccupied with sin and guilt, living in fear of punishment. The stain of original sin marks our lives. Life for us becomes a vale of tears with moments of consolation. The words of the Baltimore Catechism guide our life: "God made us to know, love, and serve Him and to be happy with Him in heaven." We now fight the good fight to be rewarded with eternal happiness in the next life.

From the perspective of a majority of believers, misery with moments of happiness now is our natural state. Lasting joy is a divine gift for the afterlife.

Fortunately, nearly a quarter of believers profess faith in a Benevolent God of mercy, love, and compassion. This group, I believe, comes closer to the heart of authentic religion in what they profess as truth. The word *gospel* means "good news." What is that good news? That God loves and cares for us every moment of our lives. He comforts us in our afflictions and forgives our failings. He remains faithful to us, even when we are unfaithful to Him. In fact, this loving God dwells in our hearts, in all of us, and in the entire universe. As St. John wrote: "God is love, and he who abides in love abides in God, and God in him." (I John 4:16)

The fruit of love is lasting joy and peace. St. Paul affirms the power of love in the midst of our earthly trials. He writes: "Who will separate us from the love of Christ? Trial, or distress, or persecution, or hunger, or nakedness, or danger, or the sword?...Yet in all this we are more than conquerors because of him who has loved us." (Romans 8: 35, 37) Those whose lives are dedicated to loving God and their neighbor wholeheartedly are promised triumph over their sufferings. Even in our sufferings we can find joy now and not only in heaven.

From the perspective of a minority of believers, misery can be overcome here and now through faith in the power of God's love. When we see His presence in ourselves, in others, and everywhere, we gain confidence, strength, and peace to live fruitful lives. In fact, the signs of authentic religion are cheerfulness, friendliness, and kindness.

REASON'S RESPONSE

"I can't get no satisfaction!" is the complaint I hear daily in my therapy room. Most of my patients come to see me because they have been on a misery-go-round for some time. They don't know how to get off. I invite them to become scientists, close observers of their lives, to understand the cause of their pain. Most believe that unpleasant events, circumstances, and people cause their suffering. However, closer examination with their wise minds reveals that it is their reaction to what is happening to them that brings them so much distress. If they are willing to dig deeper into themselves with their intelligence, I assure them, they can find a path to contentment.

Not surprisingly, our reasoned search together leads to many of the conclusions of authentic religion. Ancient wisdom affirms the overlapping of reason and faith in the pursuit of happiness and fulfillment. For example, the philosopher-Caesar, Marcus Aurelius, advises: "Dig deep; the water—goodness—is down there. And as long as you keep digging, it will keep bubbling up." (*Meditations*, 7: 59). If we dig deep enough, we discover our innate goodness, our divine likeness, not our sinfulness. Living out of our sense of goodness brings peace. Marcus Aurelius further recommends: "Go within. Nowhere you can go is more peaceful—more free of interruptions—than your own soul. Especially if you have other things to rely on. An instant's reflection and there it is: complete tranquility. And by tranquility I mean a kind of harmony." (4: 3) Peace and joy come from a sense of inner harmony with ourselves, others, and nature.

When my patients come to see me, they are torn apart by inner conflicts. Their turmoil overflows into their relationships. They are at war with themselves and long to be happy. They tell me about their problems and the dire circumstances of their lives. Then, I invite them to look inwards. I assume that they are so painfully conflicted because they are not living from their true nature, which I believe is one of happiness. So, I ask, "What keeps you from being happy?" Exploring that question, we begin the work of untangling those resistant emotional/mental knots, often caused by faulty learning from childhood and society.

When we are anxious, depressed, or angry, we sense that something is missing in our lives, robbing us of the happiness we crave. Often with a sense of desperation, my patients ask me how to find relief. I assure them that they have the answer within themselves, but don't know it. I tell them, "Just spend some time alone with yourself. Pay close attention to what emerges, and see what you learn about yourself." I invite them to undertake a fascinating and frightening journey of self-discovery.

Over time, if they take the risk to look honestly inside, they discover they cling to things that will never give them lasting joy. They look for satisfaction in the wrong places. They mourn for and fear losing what they mistakenly believe would guarantee happiness—health, status, possessions, comforts, approval, relationships, and so forth. Their pursuits may not match the largeness of their heart's desires. Yet they resist giving up these familiar satisfactions. Disappointment inevitably follows the clinging.

They also begin to listen to the deeper longings of their heart for lasting peace and joy, without limits. The highest truth, the noblest beauty, the purest goodness fascinate them, and they cannot settle for less. They discover their deepest desire to love and be loved, perfectly and forever. It dawns on them that only by dedicating themselves to their ultimate concerns will they be set free. I tell them, "Those longings express your true nature. Now what can you do to feel more alive?"

Both reason and authentic religion point in the same direction. Our fulfillment and lasting delight can only be found in living out of our ultimate concerns, our highest values, following the angels of our better nature. We may suffer for being true to our convictions, but we will still feel an underlying joy. In the end, it is all-inclusive love that satisfies our deepest aspirations.

THE JOY OF LOVING

Pursuing happiness is like chasing the wind. If sought directly, it eludes us. In reality, contentment is a byproduct of living a good life, however we personally define it. Reason and religion suggest that the pinnacle of a good life is one lived in selfless love. Love brings us lasting joy, as even the romance novels testify. Misery, on the other hand, results from being alienated from ourselves and others.

Authentic love arises from a realization of the common life we share with one another. Let me offer some suggestions for cultivating a sense of belonging with others and finding joy:

Pay it forward:

We Americans take pride in being rugged individuals who raise ourselves up by our bootstraps. In reality, however, we stand on the shoulders of others. A moment's reflection reveals how are lives have been shaped by the contributions of countless individuals—family, friends, teachers, and others. So many have enriched our lives, enabling us both to survive and thrive. We need to take time daily to remember even the small acts of kindness and service we have received from others that day. That recollection will inspire gratitude, which in turn, will motivate us to be generous. Then, we will find ways of paying it forward from the abundance we have already received.

Keep balanced:

We all entertain high expectations for our lives and suffer many disappointments. Eventually, we learn that everything, whatever happens to us and whatever we do, is both a blessing and a curse at the same time. We feel cursed when we get what we want and blessed when we do not. If our immediate preferences rule our lives, we will feel tossed about on a stormy sea, barely keeping afloat. However, if we learn to accept whatever comes with patience, attuned to the hidden blessing, we can steady the boat. We can keep our eyes on the horizon and guide our lives to our desired distant shore. There we find peace.

Love your fate:

We all share a common lot in life. We are subject to fate, events beyond our control. Some happenings please us, while others do not. We instinctively react to what happens to us with a sense of helplessness. Even though we have little control over our fate, we are always free in how we respond. For example, if we become ill, we may hate it. But the fact does not change. We are still sick, and additionally feel miserable about it. However, if we embrace our illness, and even love it, we may be surprised at what we learn. St. Paul reminds us, "We know that God makes all things work together for the good for those who love Him." (Romans 8: 28) We can love God through our sickness and offer it up to Him. Then, even illness can be an occasion of intimacy with God and joy.

Cultivate compassion:

All of us want to be happy and avoid suffering. However, none of us can escape suffering because we live in a world in which everything passes away. We are born to die, and to lose everyone and everything we hold dear. Our lives become an endless series of attachments and losses. Grief is built into our nature. That can be a cause of lament or joy, depending on how we respond. Our inevitable losses may make us either bitter or better. They can either close or open our hearts. Through our suffering, we can develop a tender heart that reaches out to others in compassion. Our mutual support in our shared sufferings can create lasting bonds of love and joy in life.

Have sympathetic joy:

We all experience joys and sorrows, often in alternating periods. If we are sad, just wait. Happiness is around the corner. If we are happy, the mood can change in an instant. Times of joy may seem rare, and therefore precious to us. So we cling to those moments. When we see others happy, we may become jealous, especially in our dark moods. We want what they have. However, if we recognize the life we share with all, their joys and sorrows are also ours. As we commiserate with them in their difficult times, we can rejoice with them in their good times. Imagine how our joy increases if we sympathize with the happy moments of all around us.

"Life is a comedy to those who think, a tragedy to those who feel," the French dramatist Jean Racine famously observed. We all experience the tragedy of life. No one escapes. At times our sorrows and fears may be so intense and prolonged that we come to believe that misery is our natural state. We believe distress is our only destiny. However, if we dare to dive deeply into our experience with an open mind and sincere faith, we discover that the heart of the universe is love. By living in love we come to know ourselves and the God of love. And in love we find lasting joy.

CHAPTER TWENTY EIGHT

ADVENT KNOWING

"Blessed are the pure of heart for they shall see God."
—Jesus of Nazareth

We Catholics see ourselves as an advent people who seek to know the presence of God in our daily lives.

The message of Advent is clear and concise: "Awake from sleep. Christ, the Light of the World, is coming. Prepare the way of the Lord." This direct command contains a wealth of guidance for both the spiritual and psychological paths, towards holiness, fullness of life, and joy. Awakening to the presence of God in our lives fulfills who we are as persons. In finding God, we discover our true selves.

ROLE MODELS

The first step on the path is a decision: either sleep in ignorance or awake in knowledge. It is a choice between life and death, between freedom and slavery.

The Advent readings present models of both fateful decisions. Herod was greatly disturbed when the magi from the east came and asked him, "Where is the newborn king of the Jews?" After consulting with the chief priests and scribes, Herod hatched a plan to destroy his perceived competitor. He asked the magi to report to him the child's whereabouts, "that I too may go and pay him homage." Herod lied, embracing falsehood, rather than truth. His true intent was to kill the newborn child because he believed him to be a threat to his power. Herod remained asleep in ignorance. He preferred to live in darkness. His fear eventually erupted in violence, slaughtering the innocent children of the area.

In contrast, Mary, Joseph, and John the Baptist exemplify those thirsting to know the truth. They had the purity of heart to see God when He revealed Himself. The angel Gabriel visited Mary and announced, "Hail, full of grace! The Lord is with you....Behold, you will conceive in your womb and bear a son." Mary was perplexed but trusted the divine messenger's word. She responded, "Behold, I am the handmaid of the Lord. May it be done to me according to your word." She surrendered in faith to the truth revealed to her.

Joseph was likewise disturbed and perplexed when he found out that Mary was pregnant. He decided to divorce her quietly to avoid exposing her to shame. Then, an angel appeared to him in a dream and said, "Joseph, son of David, do not be afraid to take Mary your wife into your home. For it is through the Holy Spirit that this child has been conceived in her." Despite his misgivings, Joseph awoke and took Mary into his home, as the angel commanded. He trusted the angel's truthful word.

John the Baptist saw his mission in life to prepare the way of the Lord. However, he was not sure who the Messiah was. While in prison, he sent his disciples to Jesus with this question, "Are you the one who is to come, or should we look for another." Jesus said in reply, "Go and tell John what you hear and see." They observed all the marvelous healings and teachings of Jesus. When John saw Jesus later, he exclaimed, "Look! There is the Lamb of God who takes away the sins of the world." John believed in the signs of God's presence displayed in Jesus' deeds and words.

The second step on the path is a willingness to prepare the way of the Lord in our hearts. That requires removing any obstacles to our recognizing and embracing the truth of God's presence. To see clearly, we have to remove our blinders.

Herod refused to acknowledge Jesus as the long-awaited Emmanuel, God with us. He was preoccupied with preserving his own earthly power and could not look beyond his self-interest. He unquestionably believed that the coming Messiah posed a political threat. Power became his god. His thirst for power and status blinded him to the truth of who Jesus the Christ was. He was unwilling to clear a path in his heart to receive his unrecognized Savior.

In contrast, Mary, Joseph, and John show us the way to prepare our hearts to receive our Lord. They opened their minds and hearts to the unexpectedly new. Their faith was not blind, though. They asked questions and confronted their doubts and illusions. Mary was greatly troubled at the angel Gabriel's praises of her. She became even more perplexed when the angel announced that she would bear a son. Refusing to be submissive, Mary asked, "How can this be, since I have no relations with a man?" When the angel explained that the power of the Most High would overshadow her, Mary let go of her confusion and doubts. She accepted a truth she could not fully comprehend.

In a similar way, Joseph shared Mary's confusion and doubts about his betrothed's unexpected pregnancy. His doubts led him to plan a secret divorce. The reassurance of the appearance of an angel in his dream gave him the courage to face his fears and doubts. He did not ignore his reservations but surrendered them to what he believed was a greater truth revealed to him.

John the Baptist knew he had a divinely-given mission, but he did not know where it would lead. He lived a life of self-renunciation in the desert, dressed in camel's hair and eating grasshoppers and wild honey. He proclaimed a baptism of repentance. John personally lived a life of repentance so that he was ready to recognize Jesus as the Son of God when he came to be baptized by him.

ADVENT PEOPLE

We are an advent people who seek to know the presence of God in our daily lives. The eternal God has not come just once in the birth of Jesus in Bethlehem. He comes to us every moment of our lives, seeking to be born in our hearts.

Jesus, as the revelation of God, comes as the Light of the world to dispel its darkness. He is the Way, the Truth, and the Life we all seek in the depths of our hearts. In our spiritual journeys, we first seek to love God with our whole hearts and minds. Next, we prepare the way by getting rid of any attachments that keep God from being our first love. Jesus announced this 2-step process when he began his public teaching. He proclaimed, "This is the time of fulfillment. The reign of God is at hand! Reform your lives and believe the good news." We can believe in God's love only if we first reform our lives.

As a first step, we decide whether or not we want to know and live by the Highest Truth, who is God. God always seems to be playing a game of hide and seek with us. He comes to us in unexpected ways, as He did with Mary, Joseph, and John. He gives us signs of his love in the love of others. Nature reveals His majesty and beauty. He may come in dreams and intuitions that ring true in our hearts. If we believe in God's constant loving care and guidance, we are attuned to these hidden signs of His Presence.

In order to be attuned to His Presence in these signs, we must want to know and love Him with our whole being. For example, a student asked his teacher how much he must want enlightenment, to know God. The teacher took him to a lake and held his head under water. The student flailed to catch his breath. After the teacher released the student from the water, he told him, "You must want to know God as much as you want to breathe." In short, the love of God and His Truth must be our ultimate concern.

Many think that we only pray when we believe. The reverse seems to be truer. We cannot come to faith, to trust in God's love, unless we pray. We need to spend time alone in silence to listen to God speaking within our hearts. Praying means paying full attention to what is going on within and around us. We stop to reflect on the deeper meaning of what is hidden in plain sight. Then we can discern the subtle signs of His love.

In the second step, we decide whether or not we want to reform our lives, give up our attachments. These attachments become little gods for us that prevent us from knowing and loving the eternal God. If we are not fully aware of ourselves, these little gods take possession of our souls. Our conscious and hidden desires demand obedience and subservience. For example, we may desire possessions, power, status, pleasure, praise, fame, success, and so forth. If these natural desires become excessive, they become deadly sins that enslave us and keep us from loving God whole-heartedly. There are no half-measures. We cannot love God half-heartedly. So, each night I pray, "Cleanse me of my unknown faults."

This second step requires a dying to self, the same self-emptying that gave birth to God in human form. Paul recommends that we assume the attitude of Christ: "Though he was in the form of God, he did not deem equality with God as something to be grasped at. Rather, he emptied himself and took the form of a slave, being born in the likeness of men." (Phil. 2: 6-7). Instead of trying proudly to play God, we need to be more God-like in our humility.

PSYCHOLOGICAL WHOLENESS

The path to psychological health mirrors the way to spiritual growth. First, we need to make knowing our true self our life's passion. Second, we prepare ourselves by confronting any obstacles to an accurate self-knowledge. We mature as we grow increasingly in self-awareness and act on this knowledge.

When patients come to see me, they are in mental and emotional distress. They want immediate relief. Often, they expect me to magically cure them. They say, "You are the expert. Fix me." I tell them, "You have the solution within yourself. When you understand yourself, you will know what to do."

I confront them with the first step toward psychological wellbeing. I give them a choice, "Do you want to pursue the path of self-awareness or the path of ignorance? Do you want to know yourself or not?" My patients often ask me for exercises to improve their lives. I tell them to do only one thing, "Spend time alone with yourself. Observe what emerges, and we'll talk about what you discover in our sessions." Often, that is a difficult task. There are so many distractions—work, obsessions, entertainment, busy schedules—that keep them on the path of ignorance, of avoiding themselves. They may also fear what they will discover, imagining something terrible. Or they may not be willing to work so hard to gain self-knowledge, preferring the easy comfort of doing the same thing over and over.

Of course, my patients want to be happy. I tell them, "Pursuing happiness is like chasing the wind. You'll never catch it. Happiness is a byproduct of simply being your true self. So, you have to know yourself and take yourself seriously to be happy." To begin therapy, they decide whether or not to embark on the perilous and wonderful journey of self-discovery.

At the end of the process, I believe as a faith-filled person, that in discovering our true self we meet God. We are made in the image and likeness of God, and God dwells in our hearts.

The work of therapy also pursues the second path of removing obstacles to our self-awareness and happiness. I remind my patients that joy is our natural state. If we are miserable, we are causing it ourselves. I tell my patients, "Let's together try to find what keeps you from being happy." We then together examine their self-defeating reacting, thinking, and behaving. When we are unhappy, often some distorted ideas and desires, clinging to old wounds, and harmful habitual behaviors are the cause. Together we explore the outmoded reactions and thinking from childhood and later painful experiences that dominate their lives. These reactions keep them from living fully in the present moment. Through this process, my patients discover that they have developed a false sense of self that drains them of their energy. That distorted self-image keeps them from knowing and loving who they really are as ordinary human beings.

In short, I am telling my patients what Jesus proclaimed 2000 years ago, "Reform your lives and believe the good news." I create an environment for them to reshape their lives by unlearning what did not work for them from the past and by expanding their consciousness. Then they can believe the good news of their own essential goodness, wisdom, and bravery. After all, we all are the beloved of God.

Christ, the Light of the world, has come, and keeps coming. We aspire to be enlightened, to see reality as it is, not as we wish it to be. We long to let the Divine Light in and transform our lives. In the process, we remove any impurities, any distorting desires and views, that obscure our clear vision. Seeing our true selves and the Divine Presence brings us the lasting joy our hearts yearn for.

CHAPTER TWENTY NINE

CHRISTMAS LOVE

"God so loved the world that he gave his only Son…"
—John 3: 16

At Christmas, we Catholics celebrate the mystery of God's love, which lasts and never fails.

Christmas proclaims a message of peace and joy. Every Christmas card, advertizing, and TV show present some version of this message. "Joy to the world, the Lord has come!" we sing in church and while caroling. We celebrate this spirit at all our family gatherings. It is a message we are desperate to hear in our world so stained by turmoil, sadness and despair.

At this time of year, we are like the shepherds who heard the angel proclaim, "Do not be afraid; for behold, I proclaim to you good news of great joy that will be for all people. For today in the city of David a savior has been born for you who is Christ and Lord." We are reminded that Jesus is the reason for the season. We join with the multitude of heavenly hosts who praise God saying, "Glory to God in the highest and on earth peace to those on whom his favor rests." (Luke 2: 10-14)

Peace and joy may seem to be at the core of Christmas. Certainly, their importance cannot be overlooked, especially when consumerism threatens to consume the holiday spirit. However, I believe these qualities are not really the heart of the matter we celebrate. They are a byproduct and expression of its true center and source. The heart of Christmas is love. "God so loved the world that he gave his only Son, that whoever believes in him may not die but may have eternal life." (John 3: 16) Peace and joy radiate from genuine love, like the rays of the sun.

DOLORES' STORY

The Christmas holiday season is especially difficult for those who are experiencing sadness, loss, and tragedy. The Hallmark movies bring a painful contrast to their experience. The more they hear about peace and joy, the more they slide into the depths of their sadness and distress.

For example, Dolores came to see me for therapy recently. She was being strangled in the grip of grief since her adult son died of cancer in the past year. "I dread the holidays. I barely have the energy to get out of bed," she lamented. "I don't know how I'll be able to survive," she added. As Dolores related her tragic story, I thought to myself, she was well-named. Dolores means "sorrow." This poor woman was indeed a lady of sorrows, perhaps like Mary, our blessed mother.

She told me she was raised in a loveless household. Her father was a self-absorbed, demanding man. He controlled their home with his temper tantrums. He demanded constant adulation from my patient and her two sisters. Dolores desperately tried to please him, but never succeeded to fill the emptiness of his life. Her mother was subservient to her father and often withdrew into depression. Dolores said, "I never felt good enough. I saw myself as unlovable."

As a teenager, she married to escape the suffocating atmosphere of her home. She married her high school sweetheart, who was more interested in getting high on drugs than having a relationship. As she did with her father, Dolores devoted herself to caring for and pleasing him.

Her redemption came when she gave birth to her child, who immediately became the love of her life. Her husband never wanted any children and left the parenting entirely up to her. As her son grew up, they formed an inseparable bond. She felt loved for the first time in her life.

When her son was diagnosed with terminal cancer, Dolores refused to believe it. She nursed him for two years, always believing a miracle would happen. When he finally died, after weeks of terrible suffering, Dolores thought her life was over. She told me, "I feel like a failure because I couldn't keep him alive. I keep going over what I did wrong. I don't deserve to live!" Dolores felt robbed of any peace or joy in her life. Her savage self-criticism tore her apart. I asked her, "Where did your love go?" She responded, "It died with my son." I reminded her, "You would never experience such deep sadness if you did not know love."

She continues to walk courageously in the darkness of her grief, searching again for the light of love.

LOVE LASTS

Peace and joy come and go, but love lasts. It never fails. After listing several virtues, Paul writes, "There are in the end three things that last: faith, hope, and love, and the greatest of these is love." (I Corinthians 13: 13). All the virtues radiate from love like the spokes of a wheel. The wheel of love keeps rolling on through the roughest terrains of life.

In fact, even sadness and despair can be overcome by love. Ram Das, a spiritual teacher, gathered stories about his master, Neem Karoli Baba, a well-known Hindu saint. He recalled one incident: "Maharajji asked an Indian girl four times, 'Do you like sorrow or joy?' Each time the girl answered, 'I've never known joy, Maharajji, only sorrow.' Finally, Maharajji said, 'I love sorrow. It brings me closer to God.'" (*Miracle of Love*, compiled by Ram Dass, Santa Fe: Hanuman Foundation, 1995, p. 151)

For those who believe, nothing can separate us from the love of God, not even death. In fact, anything that happens in our lives, even the most unwanted events, can be an avenue to intimacy with God.

Love has no beginning or end, is so resilient, because it shares in the eternity of God. God is called by many names in all the religious traditions. Islamic believers have 99 names for God, which overlap with many Christian designations: the Merciful, the Almighty, the Most High, for example. For us Christians, though, the supreme, all-encompassing name for God is love. Our God is not solitary, detached. The Divine is a Trinity of Persons in perfect communion through love. St. John writes, "We have come to know and to believe in the love God has for us. God is love, and he who abides in love abides in God, and God in him." (I John 4: 16) Through love, we share in God's life and perfection.

LOVE CREATES LIFE

Love creates life. As the good shepherd, Jesus said, "I came that they might have life and have it to the full." (John 10: 10) He also called himself "the Way, the Truth, and the Life." His teachings and example showed the way to the fullness of life. He emptied himself in caring for others. He taught that unless we die to ourselves, like a grain of wheat, we would not bear fruit. His way of love revealed the inner workings and pattern of the universe.

God did not first take flesh with the birth of Jesus, the Christ. The universe began as an act of love and became an incarnation of God, His body. God left His splendid isolation and emptied Himself to create an other to love, our universe. His love is the energy that shapes the sun, the moon, the stars, and our planet. The universe is continuously being built by the endless combination of disparate parts. Love's attraction formed the atom, which became the molecule, which became the living cell. Love brings everything together and to life. The miracle of life occurred when the molecules became complex and large enough to sustain life. Then the plants, insects, animals, and all living creatures were born from the minerals of the earth. Mimicking divine love, all living creatures instinctively began congregating for survival.

After a long preparation, the greatest miracle was the coming of us humans, with the birth of reflective thought. Our consciousness alters our relationships with the material world. We are not merely its passive observer or victim. We are co-creators with God in renewing the earth. Our planet is not an extended flat surface, as we once thought. It is a globe with limited space. Consequently, we are all interdependent on this spaceship earth. We cannot avoid interacting with each other or sharing a common destiny. Our survival depends on loving one another wisely and well. It also requires us to continually expand our consciousness to meet the challenges of an ever-changing world.

THE FLOWERING OF LOVE

The overflowing love of the Father, Son, and Holy Spirit not only creates the universe but also it is the source and model for our loving one another. We are made in the image and likeness of this triune God. The Divine life flows through us, and we only need not interfere with its expression. We are not isolated individuals but programmed to survive and thrive by creating community. Like God, our loving concern is not only for our fellow human beings, but for our whole world, which is a sacrament of God's presence. Like God, our love is not exclusive. We love all, including our enemies and even ourselves when we think ourselves most unlovable.

St. Paul expresses the breadth and depth of love in his famous hymn to love: "Love is patient; love is kind. Love is not jealous, it does not put on airs, it is not snobbish. Love is never rude, it is not self-seeking, it is not prone to anger; neither does it brood over injuries. Love does not rejoice in what is wrong but rejoices with the truth. There is no limit to love's forbearance, to its trust, its hope, its power to endure." (I Corinthians 13: 4-7)

Authentic love is multifaceted. It includes all the virtues. It honors others as we wish to be honored as children of God. Love is always a free gift, expecting no return. Cultivating love will inevitably blossom into the peace and joy our hearts long for in the Christmas season.

During Christmas, we celebrate the mystery of God's love for us. He first created our world and us to be the bearer of his love. Then, he sent his Son to share our humanity and remind us of who we are. God's love resides in our hearts and yearns to be expressed. All our deepest longings will be satisfied as the offspring of that love.

CHAPTER THIRTY

GIFT EXCHANGE

"The people who walked in darkness have seen a great light."
—Isaiah 9: 1

We Catholics believe that God reveals Himself in Jesus Christ, in creation, in the Church, and is us.

"I'm so exhausted! I can't wait until the holidays are over," adults complain. The Christmas season is filled with toil and trouble. Adults are fatigued with the endless round of decorating, cooking, baking, partying, gift buying and wrapping, and fighting crowds at the mall.

"I'm so excited! I can't wait until Christmas comes," exclaim children. They are excited to be on vacation, escaping the toil and trouble of school. Play time begins, and they look forward to Santa coming. They enjoy the rounds of parties, time with friends, caroling, meeting Santa, and getting gifts.

Both the giving and receiving, the toil and excitement, capture the true spirit of Christmas—and make the world go around. God gives the gift of Himself in His Son. We open-heartedly receive that great gift and respond by sharing ourselves with God and one another. The freely given gift exchange creates a bond of love.

COMING OF THE MAGI

The Christmas season ends with the Feast of Epiphany. The word "epiphany" means manifestation, disclosure, showing. God shows himself to the whole world in the birth of His Son, Jesus, the Light of the world. The magi, wise men from the east, follow a star to Jesus' crib. Matthew wrote: "They were overjoyed at seeing the star, and on entering the house they saw the child with Mary his mother. They prostrated themselves and did him homage. Then, they opened their treasures and offered gifts of gold, frankincense, and myrrh." (Matthew 2: 10-11) These enlightened wise men followed the light of a star. They trusted it would lead them to the Source of all light. They were not disappointed.

How did the magi respond to their discovery? First, they were overjoyed at the privilege of being led to Jesus, the newborn King of the Jews— and of the universe. Their hearts were filled with gratitude. They were the few chosen to witness this epiphany. They realized they were receiving a great gift. These were wise men who dedicated their lives to the search for wisdom, for light in the midst of darkness. Now, their deepest longings were being realized.

Next, they bowed down and paid Jesus homage. They initially came to honor a newborn king. However, they came to believe that they were in the presence of the Divine. They sensed the sacred in this ordinary place. The humble stable became for them a magnificent temple. The manger on which Jesus lay was transformed into an altar. It was an altar of worship destined to be one of sacrifice.

Finally, their gratitude and faith inspired generosity. They opened their treasure chests and offered carefully selected gifts. They presented gold fit for a king, frankincense to honor a God, and myrrh to prepare Jesus for his burial. As any loving gift-giver, they wanted to please the recipient. In their wisdom, they were attuned to who this newborn child truly was. Their gifts recognized his true nature and destiny.

Our Christmas practice of gift-giving originated with the magi. St. Nicholas (Santa Claus) walked in their footsteps centuries later. The wise men knew, as we learned from them, that the heart-felt exchange of gifts is a powerful expression of love. It creates and nourishes the bond of love. It establishes community, fulfilling Jesus' prayer, "that all may be one as you, Father, are one in me, and I in you: I pray that they may be one in us." (John 17:21)

FOLLOWING THE STAR

The magi are also called astrologers. They watched the stars and their changing patterns. By observing nature closely, they hoped to uncover the eternal wisdom hidden beneath the changing appearances. One night they observed a bright star arising and saw a glimpse of something extraordinary. They perceived a glimmer of divine light and undertook a journey to find its Source. For them, nature was the first epiphany of God's presence.

The ancient wise elders observed, and science today has confirmed, that our immense universe is relational. Everything is interdependent, from the atom to human beings. Objects are not as solid and separate as they appear. Everything is a composition of parts. Our vast universe gives and receives from far and wide a diversity of parts to make a whole. It is one gigantic gift-exchange. For example, the atom mirrors outer space. It is a nucleus with whirling electrons and subatomic particles in open space, which unite with other atoms. Matter is energy crystallized in ever- changing patterns. That energy is also ordered to create forms, suggesting the presence of intelligence.

Driven by that intelligent energy, our earth has evolved over millions of years. Over time, the parts making the whole have become more complex and unified. Atoms and molecules accumulate to form living cells. These cells further congregate to form the nearly countless living creatures that inhabit our planet—plants, bacteria, insects, fish, birds, animals, and so forth. The final living form is us human beings. Evolution took a major leap with the birth of reflective thought. And our consciousness is still evolving. Its peak is the recognition of the Divine always and everywhere. The magi showed that higher consciousness in seeing the Light of the World in Jesus.

Other sages, like the magi, perceived God's presence throughout the process of evolution. Some perceived nature as cyclical, like the seasons. Others saw it as progressing in a straight line to a final end. On the one hand, Hindu sages view nature as an eternal cycle of constant repetition until a final liberation and union with the Supreme Reality. The Gods are always within and beyond unfolding nature. Brahma the Creator, Vishnu the Preserver, and Shiva the Destroyer operate through all the cycles of change as the underlying Source and Power.

On the other hand, the Jewish-Christian tradition views nature from a historical perspective. History moves in a straight line according to God's plan to its final fulfillment. Perhaps, it is more accurate to say we move in a slow upward spiral, with some side trips. We believe Christ is the Center of history, the Beginning and End. He is like the nucleus of the atom of life. St. Paul wrote: "He (Christ) is the image of the invisible God, the first-born of all creatures. In him everything in heaven and earth was created....He is before all else that is. In him everything continues in being." (Colossians 1: 15-17) His presence energizes our move forward.

In God's plan, the evolution of the planet continues through those chosen ones who believe in Him. St. Paul wrote: "God chose us in him before the world began, to be holy and blameless in his sight, to be full of love....God has given us the wisdom to understand fully the mystery, the plan he was pleased to decree in Christ, to be carried out in the fullness of time: namely, to bring all things in the heavens and on earth into one under Christ's headship." (Ephesians 1: 4, 9-10) We have been chosen as the growing edge of evolution through our expanding consciousness and love for one another. We are co-creators with God of a better world.

The final goal of history and nature, however, is the same for Hindus and Christians: a perfect communion of life and love with God, one another, and all creation.

BEING THE LIGHT

His disciples proclaimed Jesus the Light of the World. In turn, Jesus taught that we too are bearers of that light. He said, "You are the light of the world. A city set on a hill cannot be hidden. Men do not light a lamp and then put it under a bushel basket. They set it on a stand where it gives light to all in the house." (Matthew 5: 14-15) We are called to be the final epiphany for a world shrouded in darkness. That is really what the Church is meant to be: the sacrament of His presence in the world today. How are we to accomplish such a noble and daunting task? The magi suggest a way:

Be Seekers:

The magi were stargazers, alert for signs of the sacred. They courageously undertook a journey into the unknown by following the star. They had no idea where it would take them, or what dangers and challenges would await them. Their yearning for the light of truth inspired their search. Their belief in the Light carried them along. In the same way, we must have the same passion for wisdom and alertness for what is true. The search will inevitably lead us into unknown regions. It will be necessary to face with courage our fear of the dark. Joseph Campbell, the American expert on myth, said, "The cave you fear most to enter holds your greatest treasure."

Be Grateful:

Open to the unexpected, the magi received everything they experienced as a wondrous gift. Their hearts were filled with gratitude. In contrast, many of us entertain many high expectations about our lives and are easily disappointed. We feel entitled. Or we imagine that we earn everything we have. However, only a moment's reflection will reveal how much we stand on the shoulders of others and how much others depend on us. What do we have that has not been given to us—our life, health, relationships, abilities, and so forth? Everything is grace. Gratitude opens our hearts to generosity, to seeking a way to pay back.

Be Reverent:

The magi's first instinct in meeting the newborn Jesus was to prostrate themselves and do him homage. Pride did not blind them to the mystery of the moment. They immediately perceived they were in the presence of the Divine. In the same way, a fully conscious love recognizes the divine dignity of the recipients of our gifts.

Mother Teresa, the saint of Calcutta, was often asked what motivated her care for the poorest of the poor. She said, "I am not a social worker. Everything I do is for the love of God." Then, she held up her hand and repeated the words of Jesus at the last judgment in Matthew's Gospel. With each word she raised a finger, saying, "You do this for me." She explained that she sees Christ in everyone she serves. We are all "another Christ."

The Hindus have a greeting that expresses this same sacred awareness. When they greet one another, they bow their heads with folded hands and say, "Namaste." The gesture and expression mean, "The Divine in me honors the Divine in you."

<u>Be Generous:</u>

Gratitude and faith in the divine presence motivated the magi's giving gifts. Generosity naturally overflows from gratitude. Love is further deepened by the recognition of the sacredness of the other. In a similar way, we give to others out of an awareness of our own abundance, of how much we have already received. We do not begrudgingly give out of our poverty. Love abounds and has a multipier effect for both the giver and receiver. It is never lost or diminished. Love grows in the sharing of ourselves. It creates new life and unbreakable bonds.

The Feast of Epiphany celebrates the showing of God's presence in creation, in the birth of Jesus, and in all humanity. The divine Light has shined in the darkness of our world. The magi followed the star to the crib of Jesus, the newborn King. They are the star that lights our way to the joyful finding of God's wondrous love. They invite us to a gift exchange which will result in a life-giving communion with God, one another, and all creation.

CHAPTER THIRTY ONE

A NEW YEAR

"May it be done to me according to your word."
—Luke 1: 38

We Catholics believe we are co-creators with God of the future, which unfolds according to His will.

A new year begins. The transition between the past and the coming year invites reflection. We all look back and then forward. Commentators review the best and worst of everything, attempt to discern trends, and make predictions for the coming year. Will it be a good or bad year— the best of times or the worst of times? Who really knows?

Nevertheless, commentators make their prognostications, sometimes with great confidence. Of course, their opinions vary. Many are diametrically opposed, as if they are looking at different universes. I suspect their imagined futures are really a projection of their own idiosyncratic views of themselves and the world. After all, we see others as we are.

As we begin a new year, of course, we take a personal look at our lives. We look back at our regrets and celebrations. Inevitably, our lives have been a mixed bag. We then look to the next year and entertain expectations about what will occur. Finally, we make New Year's resolutions. How can I become a better person? What do I need to do? That is a familiar annual exercise.

As the year begins, we naturally entertain expectations about the coming year. Those expectations guide our choices. They give us a sense of direction and control over our destiny. We then set goals and objectives accordingly. Our views of the future shape our lives, often more than we imagine. Who we are emerges from the way we think about ourselves and the trajectory of our lives.

Have you ever stopped to consider how you view the future? On what do you base your projections? Are you a pessimist, optimist, or realist? Most of us fall into one of these three categories. However, such thinking about the future can limit us. It can interfere with our living fully the present moment.

Is there another way to view the coming year, without preconceptions, open to whatever comes?

On January 1, the Catholic Church celebrates the Feast of Mary, the Mother of God. She is our model for an alternative attitude. After the birth of her son and hearing the stories of the magi and shepherds, Luke recounted, "And Mary kept all these things, reflecting on them in her heart." (Luke 2: 16) She reflected and responded with the openness she showed with the angel Gabriel, "Behold, I am the handmaid of the Lord. May it be done to me according to your word." (Luke 1: 38) She accepted with trust the angel's invitation to become pregnant, not understanding where it would lead.

OUR IMAGINED FUTURES

Let us begin by looking at our ordinary thinking about the future. We cannot help but have expectations, which reflect our wishes. Most of these ideas, however, are based on past experience and how we interpret it. As I mentioned above, most of us tend to think in these three predictable patterns:

Pessimists:

"Pessimists are never disappointed," we tell ourselves. This view arises from many past experiences of disappointment, which we expect to continue. Our hopes have been dashed, and we suffered great pain as a result. Perhaps at one time we entertained high expectations for ourselves and others, but the disappointment was too much for us. We decided never to aim so high again. So, we are always preparing ourselves for the worst. We live defensively, in anticipation of some disaster. We tell ourselves, "I won't let anything defeat me again!" We may feel safe. However, the price we pay for such a worldview is a loss of joy. We do not live fully the present moment and never learn to appreciate the simple joys of life.

Optimists:

Optimists tell themselves, "When you're positive, good things happen. I always expect the best." We believe in the law of attraction, that goodness inevitably attracts the same, and vice versa. We believe in the power of positive thinking. That is natural for us Americans who firmly believe in progress. We are idealists at heart. We expect our lives to improve, if we work hard enough and get a few breaks. We also believe in the value of hard work to overcome all obstacles. Such optimism can inspire great achievements. However, when we hit a wall, and our best efforts fail, we may feel lost. We may not know how to make sense of failure, loss, defeat, or even death, which is the complete loss of control.

<u>Realists:</u>

So-called realists, who seek a balanced view of their lives, say, "I hope for the best, but prepare for the worst." We see our lives as a roller coaster with ups and downs, highs and lows. We seem to be preparing ourselves for the extremes, the best and the worst. A patient of mine who was in the Army told me he learned this attitude in order to be prepared for the unpredictability of war. He had to be ready and resourceful. Such a view arises from the experience of life as an ongoing contest with forces of good and evil. We are always preparing ourselves for a fight. We never fully relax. We are always waiting to respond to events beyond our control.

SEIZE THE MOMENT

Aside from these three natural ways of thinking, there is a fourth way. It is the way of Mary. "Let it be," she said. It is the way of living fully the present moment with an attitude of openness, beyond fear and desire. There is no need to have a clear idea or guarantee of a future outcome.

In reality, the future is always unknown. It does not yet exist. Whatever we imagine about the future is just a current thought, not reality. Thinking we know what will happen may give us the illusion of security. In the same way, all of our memories and interpretations about the past are also just thoughts, not reality. They are conditioned ways of thinking that can distract us from experiencing whatever is happening in the present moment. Only the present moment is real.

A patient of mine, who often got lost in his thoughts, would begin each session with the same question, "What's new?" I always responded, "This moment is new. In the history of the universe, it never existed and never will again." He often wanted to pick up where we left off in the last session. But I invited him to be present to whatever he experienced of himself in that moment. "Talk about whatever is on your mind," I told him.

The following are some suggestions for staying in the present moment, the only time that is real:

Be childlike:

Mary was a young teenager, a mere child, when the angel approached her. Jesus said, "Unless you become like a little child, you cannot enter the kingdom of God." We admire the innocence of children. They do not carry the burden of the past or guilt. Their history is brief, so they do not get caught up in thinking about the past. Their expectations about the future too are limited, mostly influenced by what we adults tell them. Instead, they live the present moment, often with a playful attitude. They possess a natural sense of joy, untarnished by the ravages of failure, disappointment, and resentment. In their innocence and unself-conscious enjoyment of life they are models for us.

Let go of the past:

So young, Mary was not burdened by her past or guilt. She was free to respond to the moment whole-heartedly. Our daily challenge is to avoid clinging to our views of the past. Memory can be a severe taskmaster. It can rule our lives. We may relish happy moments, but it is the tragic times that most capture our attention. By nature, we are inclined to protect ourselves from negative events, more than celebrating the positive. So we project our negativity and fear into the future.

Freedom to enjoy fully the present moment requires that we let go of our regrets and wounds from the past and not let them dominate our lives. Unfortunate events are opportunities to learn and grow. Whatever happens to us is a vehicle for our personal growth in the present. We just need to learn how to use this gift.

Be open to surprise:

Mary accepted the angel's invitation, without comprehending or asking where it would lead. In contrast, we often become prisoners of our expectations, without even knowing it. Events happen, and we think we know their meaning from past experience. However, we cannot be as confident as with think in evaluating the good or evil of events. We lack a large enough perspective.

There is a well-known Chinese story about trying to assess the future. A poor farmer's horse ran off into the country of the barbarians. All his neighbors said, "Isn't that terrible?" But the father responded, "We'll see." After a few months, the horse returned with a barbarian horse of excellent stock. All his neighbors said, "Isn't that wonderful?" But the father said, "How do you know that it isn't a disaster? We'll see." The two horses bred, and the family became rich in fine horses. The farmer's son spent much time riding and training them. Then, one day he fell off and broke his hipbone. All his neighbors said, "Isn't that terrible?" and offered their condolences. But his father responded, "How do you know that this isn't good fortune? We'll see." Another year passed, and the barbarians invaded the area. All the able-bodied young men were drafted to fight, and 9/10 of them died in the war. Who can tell how events will unfold? The only realistic response is, "We'll see."

We can never know with certainty the outcome of our decisions. However, what happens to us can always lead to some beneficial result. Being open invites us to live without regret. "Never regret a day in your life: good days give happiness, bad days give experience, worst days give lessons, and best days give memories." (Unknown source)

See God's presence:

Mary believed Gabriel who assured her that she was full of grace and that the Lord was with her at that moment. The present moment is often called the eternal now. It is the privileged time in which God reveals Himself. At Christmas, we celebrate that God became human in Jesus Christ. God took on our flesh, our history, our life. In short, we believe that God is present in our history, in every moment and event or our lives. No matter what happens, God is with us. He is both celebrating and suffering with us. We are never alone.

The God we Christians believe in is triune: Father, Son, and Holy Spirit. In every circumstance, we can sense the presence of God. When our lives are unfolding in unexpected ways, we come to know better the Father, the Creator. When we fail or suffer, we come closer to the Son, the Redeemer. When we strive to grow and become holy (whole), we are assisted by the Holy Spirit, the Sanctifier. God's grace is ever-present.

Even before the coming of Christ, the Hindus had a deep faith in the presence of God in all the circumstances of their lives. They also believed in a Trinity: Brahma, Vishnu, and Siva. Brahma is the Creator, who brings new life. Vishnu is the Preserver, whom we experience as our lives unfold. Siva is the Destroyer, whose presence we sense when our lives are falling apart. We sense the Divine working through us in all these situations. Everything is grace, under the watchful eye and care of God.

As a new year begins, we reflect on the events of the past year. We also look forward to the coming year and make resolutions. Mary is our model for reflecting and commitment-making. She showed an attitude of openness to an unknown future, unburdened by crippling expectations. She embraced the moment and trusted God in surrendering to His will. Each year we are preparing ourselves to finally embrace a new life we believe is eternal.

EPILOGUE

"Who will separate us from the love of Christ?"
—Paul of Tarsus

We Catholics, and organized religion in general, have a bad name these days. Fewer people today attend church or admit belonging to any religion. Various surveys indicate that 16-20% of Americans claim no religious affiliation. Increasingly, they prefer to identify themselves as spiritual, and not religious.

In particular, the Catholic Church has been viewed negatively. In our predominantly white, Anglo-Saxon Protestant (WASP) country, Catholics have been a persecuted minority of "Papists," considered more loyal to Rome than to our country. In recent years, the influx of minorities from Hispanic countries, who are mostly Catholic, has heightened the suspicion of members of the Roman Church. We have been viewed as closed-minded, rule-bound, guilt-ridden, and self-righteous. We have proclaimed that there is no salvation outside the Church. We have boasted that we possess the fullness of Truth.

Nevertheless, I am proud to be Catholic, as hopefully, I made clear in this book. I am a firm believer in the Church and its teachings.

However, as, again, I hope was evident in my writing, I maintain a "catholic outlook" in my interpretation of the teachings of the faith. Catholic means "all-embracing," open to all truth, wherever it may be found. An authentic catholic attitude listens to all, especially to those of differing opinions, to uncover hidden truths to expand our own consciousness. We believe that God is a great Mystery beyond the full comprehension of any individual or religious group. We search together for a fuller understanding the depths of that Mystery. The divine love in our hearts impels us to reach out to others in kindness and listen to their stories of faith.

Having a catholic outlook also means that we accept the totality of our experience as a gift from God. Everything belongs. Nothing is excluded if we want to live the fullness of life Jesus promised. God's loving presence can be discovered in the most unexpected places. We often celebrate God's love in what we find positive, joyful, pleasant, and satisfying. However, with this natural attitude, we may seek the consolations of God and miss the God of consolation who reveals Himself in surprising ways.

Moments of adversity, trial, and suffering can be privileged moments to deepen our faith and hope. When Peter objected that Jesus would have to suffer and die, Jesus sternly reprimanded him: "Get out of my sight, you satan! You are not judging by God's standards but by man's....If a man wishes to come after me, he must deny his very self, take up his cross, and follow in my steps. Whoever would preserve his life will lose it, and whoever loses his life for my sake and the gospel's will preserve it." (Mark 8: 33-35) Jesus makes it clear, as much as we hate this truth, that we *must* suffer to rise to new life. There is no option here. The promised result is new life.

My faith helps me to understand and cope with the inevitable afflictions in life. As I tried to demonstrate in the essays in this book, our faith, and that of all authentic religious traditions, offers a path of meaning through our sufferings. We believe as Christians that we share in the sufferings of Christ, and he bears our crosses with us. We never suffer alone. Our suffering is also part of God's mysterious plan of salvation for us as individuals and for the whole world (Ephesians 1: 3-10). Even the sin of Adam was called "a happy fault" because it became the occasion for God to send a Redeemer. If we accept our distressful trials as God's will and learn from them, we will find relief and be saved.

Paul puts our inevitable suffering in the larger perspective of Christ's unfailing love. He wrote: "Who will separate us from the love of Christ? Trial, or distress, or persecution, or hunger, or nakedness, or danger, or the sword?...Yet in all this we are more than conquerors because of him who has loved us. For I am certain that neither death nor life, neither angels nor principalities, neither the present nor the future, nor powers, neither height nor depth nor any other creature, will be able to separate us from the love of God that comes to us in Christ Jesus, our Lord." (Romans 8: 35, 38-39) Adversity, no matter how intense, cannot touch the eternal soul of God's beloved. His love triumphs over all, even our worst nightmares.

We suffer with hope, confident that our struggles are not in vain, but will yield a rich harvest. Jesus promised, "Unless the grain of wheat falls to the earth and dies, it remains just a grain of wheat. But if it dies, it produces much fruit." (John 12: 24)

My catholic outlook has also led me to search the wisdom of other spiritual traditions. All religions seek to increase happiness and relieve suffering. For example, the Buddhists proclaim that pain is inevitable, but suffering is optional. What they mean is that our bodies and the whole material universe are destined to break down, causing pain. They teach that we are of a nature to get sick, grow old, die, and eventually lose everyone and everything we love. However, we can freely choose how we react to that pain. We can relieve our mental, emotional, and spiritual suffering by embracing a wholesome attitude toward life, by living according to the values of our higher nature. Our virtuous acts live on.

In recognition of these profound truths, I pray each morning: "O Lord, I offer you this day all my prayers, works, joys, and sufferings." Every time I participate in the Eucharist, I offer my entire life in praise of God. Everything we experience, even our hardships, can be a worthy offering to our Lord. Acceptance in love or our unavoidable misfortunes can help us escape the widespread victim mentality that complains, blames, and indulges in self-pity.

My prayer is that in your trying times you may assume the hopeful attitude of St. Paul: "We even boast of our afflictions! We know that affliction makes for endurance, and endurance for tested virtue, and tested virtue for hope. And this hope will not leave us disappointed, because the love of God has been poured out into our hearts through the Holy Spirit who has been given to us." (Romans 5: 3-5)

NOTES

CHAPTER ONE

1. All quotes from the Hebrew and Christian Scriptures are from *The New American Bible.*

CHAPTER TWO

1. All quotes from the *Bhagavad Gita* are from Stephen Mitchell's translation. *Bhagavad Gita* (New York: Three Rivers Press, 2000).

CHAPTER FIVE

1. All quotes of Marcus Aurelius are from Gregory Hays' translation, *Meditations* (New York: Modern Library, 2002).

CHAPTER SIX

1. See Frank Snowden, *Epidemics and Society* (New Haven: Yale University Press, 2019).
2. Diana Butler Bass, *Christianity After Religion* (New York: Harper-Collins, 2012), 49.
3. Julian of Norwich, *Revelations of Divine Love,* tr. Mirabai Starr (Charlottesville: Hampton Roads, 2013).

CHAPTER SEVEN

1. See Mirabai Starr's translation.

CHAPTER EIGHT

1. Daniel Defoe, *A Journal of the Plague Year* (Monee, Il, 2020).
2. Pope Francis, *Let Us Dream: The Path to a Better Future* (New York: Simon and Schuster, 2022).

CHAPTER NINE

1. All quotes from the *Tao Te Ching* are from Stephen Mitchell's translation, *Tao Te Ching* (New York: Harper Perennial Classics, 2000).
2. All quotes from *The Way of the Bodhisattva* are from the Padmakara Translation Group, Shantideva, *The Way of the Bodhisattva* (Boston: Shambhala, 2003).

CHAPTER TEN

1. *The Autobiography of Martin Luther King, Jr.* (New York: Grand Central Publishing, 1998), 70.
2. Bandy X. Lee, *Profiles of a Nation* (New York: World Mental Health Coalition, Inc., 2020), 124.

CHAPTER ELEVEN

1. Caryll Houselander, *This War is the Passion* (Notre Dame: Ave Maria Press, 2008).

CHAPTER TWELVE

1. Elizabeth Kubler-Ross, *On Death and Dying* (New York: Simon and Schuster, 1969).
2. *The Gospel of Sri Ramakrishna* (New York: Ramakrishna-Vivekananda Center, 1942), 628.
3. *Story of a Soul: The Autobiography of St. Therese of Lisieux* (Washington, DC.: ICS Publications, 1996), 151.

CHAPTER THIRTEEN

1. See Diana Butler Bass.
2. *The Gospel of Sri Ramakrishna,* p.436.

CHAPTER FOURTEEN

1. Mark Ortman, *The Secret of Everyday Communication* (Scottsdale: Wise Owl Press, 2021).

CHAPTER FIFTEEN

1. Paramahansa Yogananda, *The Second Coming of Christ* (Los Angeles: Self-Realization Fellowship, 2004), 9.
2. See Paramahansa Yogananda, pp. 13-14.

CHAPTER TWENTY FOUR

1. Joseph Cambell, *The Business of the Gods* (Ontario: Windrose Films, Ltd., 1989), 78.

CHAPTER TWENTY SEVEN

1. Diana Butler Bass, *Christianity After Religion* (New York: HarperCollins, 2012), 49-50.

ABOUT DR. DENNIS ORTMAN

Dennis Ortman, Ph.D., is a clinical psychologist in private practice in the Detroit Metropolitan area for over thirty years, specializing in treating those with addictions and those who have suffered the trauma of infidelity. Before becoming a psychologist, he was a Catholic priest in the Archdiocese of Detroit for fourteen years. He received the doctorate in clinical psychology from the University of Detroit-Mercy and a graduate degree in theology from the Gregorian University in Rome, Italy. With graduate degrees in both psychology and theology, he works with patients on issues at the borderline between psychology and spirituality, employing a mindful approach to therapy. He authored five books on recovery from addictions and infidelity. He also lectures around the country on utilizing the wisdom of Freud and Buddha in treatment. He has three stepchildren and five step-grandchildren.

The books he has published with MSI Press have remained popular long-term as they help many people in need, and they continue to win awards:

Anger Anonymous (Book of the Year finalist)
Anxiety Anonymous (American Bookfest Best Books Award)
Depression Anonymous (Book of the Year finalist)
Life, Liberty, and COVID-19
The Pandemic and Hope (part of the MSI Press pandemic series)

His next book will be out soon
Being Catholic in Troubled Times: Strength through Faith

MSI PRESS PUBLICATIONS: SPIRITUALITY, PSYCHOLOGY, BODY/MIND/SPIRIT

A Believer-in-Waiting (Mahlou)
A Guide to Bliss (Tubali)
A Theology for the Rest of Us (Yavelberg)
An Afternoon's Dictation (Greenebaum)
Anger Anonymous (Ortman)
Anxiety Anonymous (Ortman)

Blest Atheist (Mahlou)

Christmas at the Mission (Sula)
Creative Aging (Romer & Vassiliadis)

Depression Anonymous (Ortman)
Día de Muertos (Sula)

Easter at the Mission (Sula)
El Poder de lo Transpersonal (Ustman)
Everybody's Little Book of Everyday Prayers (MacGregor)

From Deep Within (Lewis)

Healing from Incest (Henderson & Emerton)
Heart-to-Heart Resuscitation: A Memoir (Montgomery)
Heart to Heart Resuscitation: My Journal (Montgomery)
How to Argue with an Atheist (Brink)
How to Live from Your Heart (Hucknall)

God Speaks into Darkness (Easterling)
GodSway (Keathley)
Good Blood (Schaffer)

It Only Hurts When I Can't Run (Parker)
Introductory Lectures on Religious Philosophy (Sabzevary)

Jesus Is Still Passing By (Easterling)
Joshuanism (Tosto)

Lamentations of the Heart (Wells-Snith)
Learning to Feel (Girrell)
Life after Losing a Child (Romer & Young)
Life, Liberty, & COVID-19 (Ortman)
Living in Blue Sky Mind (Diedrichs)

Of God, Rattlesnakes, and Okra (Easterling)
One Family: Indivisible (Greenebaum)

Passing On (Romer)
Puertas a la Eternidad (Ustman)

Rainstorm of Tomorrow (Dong)
Road Map to Power (Husain & Husain)

Saints I Know (Sula)
Seeking Balance in an Unbalanced Time (Greenebaum)
Since Sinai (Gonyou)
Sula and the Franciscan Sisters (Sula)
Surviving Cancer, Healing People: One Cat's Story (Sula)
Surviving Freshman Year (Jones)

Tale of a Mission Cat (Sula)
The Pandemic and Hope (Ortman)
The Rise and Fall of Muslim Civil Society (Imady)
The Rose and the Sword (Bach & Hucknall)
The Seven Wisdoms of Life (Tubali)
Typhoon Honey (Girrell & Sjogren)

Weekly Soul (Craigie)

Other MSI Press
Books by Dennis Ortman

Anger Anonymous
Anxiety Anonymous
Depression Anonymous
Life, Liberty, and COVID-19
The Pandemic and Hope

MSI Press LLC
Publications in Religion
and Philosophy

A Believer-in-Waiting's First Encounters with God (Mahlou)
A Guide to Bliss: Transforming Your Life through Mind Expansion (Tubali)
A Theology for the Rest of Us (Yavelberg)
An Afternoon's Dictation (Greenebaum)
Blest Atheist (Mahlou)
Christmas at the Mission: A Cat's View of Catholic Beliefs and Customs (Sula)
Easter at the Mission: A Cat's Observation of the Paschal Mystery (Sula)
Dia de Muertos (Sula)
El Poder de lo Transpersonal (Ustman)
Everybody's Little Book of Everyday Prayers (MacGregor)
God Speaks into Darkness (Easterling)
GodSway (Keathley)

Good Blood (Schaffer)

Heart to Heart Resuscitation (Montgomery)

How to Argue with an Atheist: How to Win the Argument without Losing the Person (Brink)

How to Live from Your Heart (Hucknall)

Introductory Lectures on Religious Philosophy (Sabzevary)

Jesus Is Still Passing By (Easterling)/Study Guide edition also available

Joshuanism (Tosto)

Lamentations of the Heart (Wells-Smith)

Life after Losing a Child (Young & Romer)

Living in Blue Sky Mind: Basic Buddhist Teachings for a Happy Life (Diedrichs)

Of God, Rattlesnakes, and Okra (Easterling)

One Family: Indivisible (Greenebaum)

Overcoming the Odds (C. Leaver)

Passing On (Romer)

Puertas a la Eternidad (Ustman)

Rainstorm of Tomorrow (Dong)

Road Map to Power (Husain & Husain)

Saints I know (Sula)

Seeking Balance in an Unbalanced Time (Greenebaum)

Since Sinai (Gonyou)

Sula and the Franciscan Sisters (Sula)

Surviving Cancer, Healing People: One Cat's Story (Sula)

Surviving Freshman Year (Jones)

Tale of a Mission Cat (Sula)

The Rise and Fall of Muslim Civil Society (O. Imady)

The Seven Wisdoms of Life (Tubali)

Weekly Soul (Craigie)

When Liberty Enslaves (Aveta)

When You're Shoved from the Right, Look to Your Left: Metaphors of Islamic Humanism (O. Imady)